G. SCHIRMER EDITION OF

PATIENCE

or Bunthorne's Bride

Book by

W. S. GILBERT

Music by

ARTHUR SULLIVAN

Authentic Version Edited by

EDMOND W. RICKETT

This score contains all the dialogue

Ed. 1982

ISBN 978-0-88188-725-9

G. SCHIRMER, *Inc.*

DISTRIBUTED BY

HAL•LEONARD®
CORPORATION

7777 W. BLUEMOUND RD. P.O. BOX 13819 MILWAUKEE, WI 53213

DRAMATIS PERSONAE

Colonel Calverley	*Officers of Dragoon Guards*
Major Murgatroyd	*Officers of Dragoon Guards*
Lieut. The Duke of Dunstable	*Officers of Dragoon Guards*
Reginald Bunthorne	*A Fleshly Poet*
Archibald Grosvenor	*An Idyllic Poet*
Mr. Bunthorne's Solicitor	
The Lady Angela	*Rapturous Maidens*
The Lady Saphir	*Rapturous Maidens*
The Lady Ella	*Rapturous Maidens*
The Lady Jane	*Rapturous Maidens*
Patience	*A Dairy Maid*

Chorus of Rapturous Maidens and Officers of Dragoon Guards

ACT I—Exterior of Castle Bunthorne

ACT II—A Glade

STORY OF THE OPERA

This sprightly satire on the æsthetic craze of the eighties presents a 'Fleshly Poet'' and an ''Idyllic Poet'', Bunthorne and Grosvenor, who are rivals for the affections of the milkmaid, Patience. A train of languid ladies and their former flames, a Colonel, a Duke, and a Major, with a regiment of officers of the Dragoon Guards, complete the picture.

Patience, having been told that love must be absolutely unselfish, has to reject the perfect Grosvenor (Archibald the All-Right) and accept the very imperfect Bunthorne. This defection of their idol drives the ladies back to their military lovers, but the reunion is soon broken up by the arrival of Grosvenor, to whom they promptly transfer their adoration. Later, the baffled Bunthorne, aided by the mature Lady Jane, concocts a scheme to get rid of the interloper by means of a terrible Curse, which compels Grosvenor to give up his æstheticism and to become a quite commonplace young man.

The plan, however, recoils, as all the ladies now revert to ordinary attire, explaining that since Archibald the All-Right cannot possibly be All-Wrong, obviously æstheticism should be discarded. Patience, discovering that her Archibald is no longer perfect, promptly falls into his arms, and Bunthorne, crushed, decides to wed Jane, his one remaining adorer. However, the Duke enters, declaring that since he is a very ordinary young man, it is only fair for him to choose a lady who is distinctly plain, *viz.*, Jane, who joyfully accepts him, so that ''Nobody is Bunthorne's Bride!''

EDMOND W. RICKETT

Orchestra material may be rented
from the publishers,
G. Schirmer, Inc.
866 THIRD AVE., NEW YORK, N.Y. 10022

Patience

or

Bunthorne's Bride

W. S. Gilbert

Arthur Sullivan

Overture

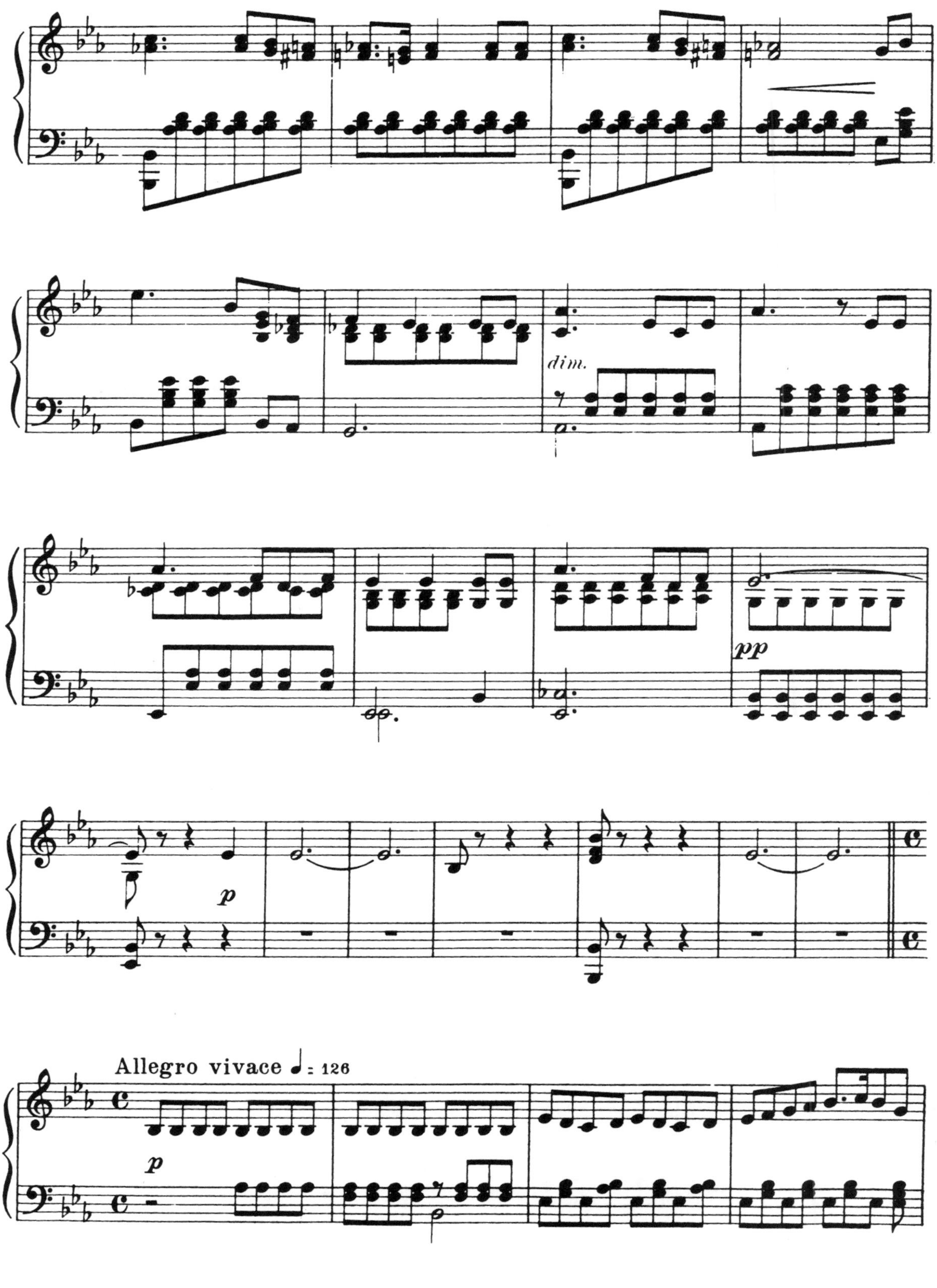
dim.
pp
p
Allegro vivace ♩= 126
p

dim.
B
pp

f
pp
f
p
cre - scen - do
pp
f
pp

ff
mf
C
pp

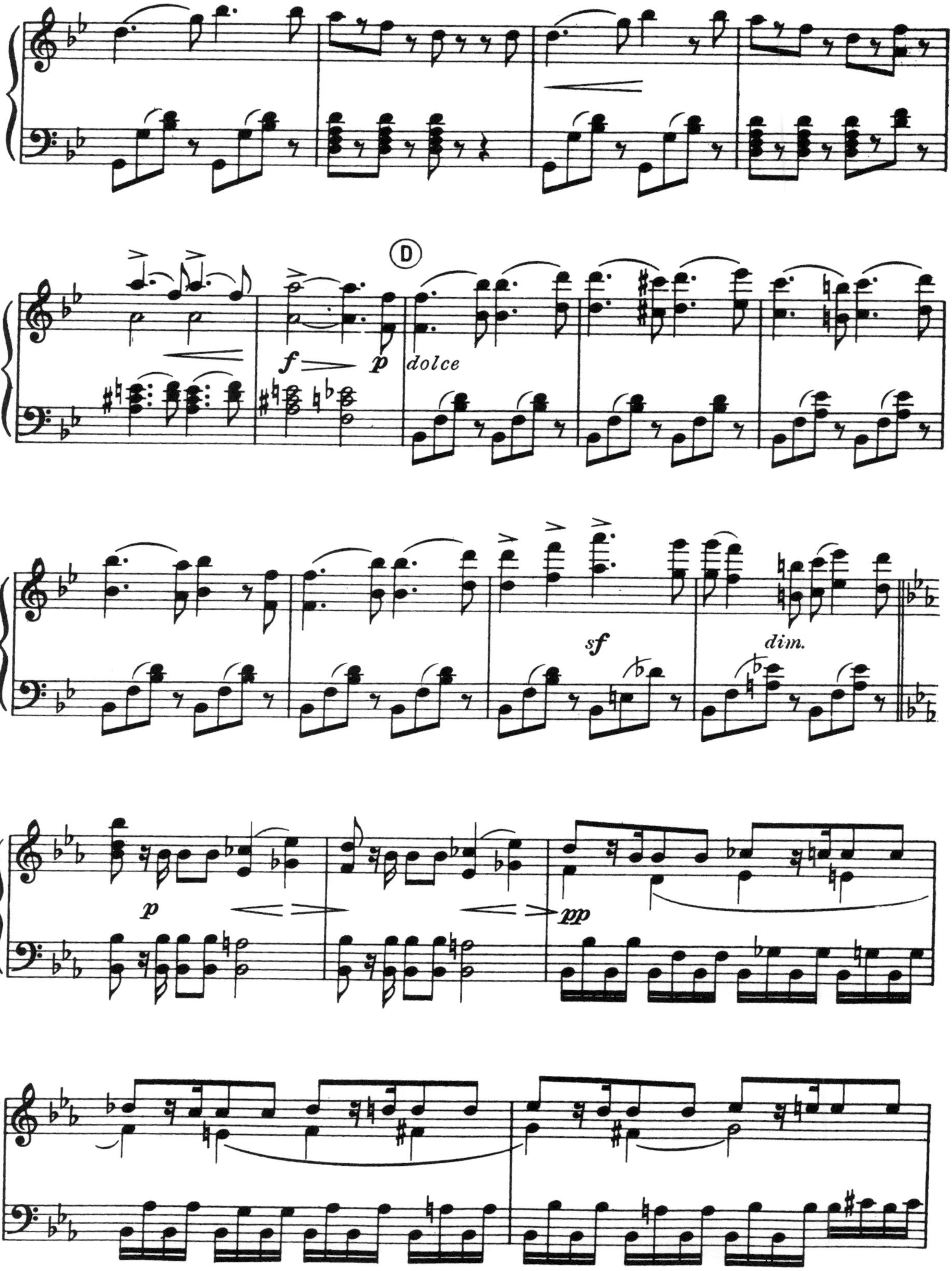
D
f
p
dolce
sf
dim.
p
pp

fz
pp
f
pp
E
ff
8

MUSICAL NUMBERS

8
p stacc.
pp
cre - scen - do
f
mf
ff

ff
8
Ped.

Act I

Scene: ***Exterior of Castle Bunthorne,*** *the gateway to which is seen,* ***R.U. E.,*** *and is approached by a drawbridge over a moat. A rocky eminence* ***R.*** *with steps down to the stage. In front of it, a rustic bench, on which* ***Angela*** *is seated, with* ***Ella*** *on her left.* ***Young Ladies*** *wearing aesthetic draperies are grouped about the stage from* ***R.*** *to* ***L.C., Saphir*** *being near the* ***L.*** *end of the group. The* ***Ladies*** *play on lutes, etc., as they sing, and all are in the last stage of despair.*

No. 1. Twenty love-sick maidens we

Opening Chorus and Solos

Maidens, Angela, and Ella

Twen-ty years hence we shall be
Twen-ty love-sick maid-ens still!
Twen - ty love-sick maid-ens we,
And we die for love of
thee!
Twen - ty love-sick maid - ens we,
Love-sick all a-gainst our will.
Twen-ty years hence we shall be
p

B
Angela
Twen-ty love-sick maid-ens still!
Love feeds on hope, they say,
p
or love will die;
Chorus
Ah, mis-er-ie!
Angela
Yet my love
lives, al-though no hope have I!
Chorus
Ah, mis-er-ie!
Angela
A-las, poor heart, go hide thy-self a-way, To

weep - ing_ con - cords tune thy roun - de - lay! Ah,
C
Chorus
mis-er-ie! All our love is all for one, Yet that love he heed-eth
not, He is coy and cares for none, Sad and sor - ry is our
lot! Ah, mis-er-ie!
D
Ella
Go, break - ing
p

heart, Go, dream of love re - quit - ed!
Go, fool - ish heart, Go, dream of lov - ers
plight - ed; Go, mad - cap heart, Go,
dream of nev - er wak - ing; And in thy

dream For-get that thou art break - ing!
Chorus
Ella
rall.
Ah, mis - er - ie! For - get that thou art break - ing!
p
colla voce
a tempo
Chorus
Twen - ty love-sick maid-ens we, Love - sick all a - gainst our
p dolce
will. Twen - ty years hence we shall be

Angela: There is a strange magic in this love of ours! Rivals as we all are in the affections of our Reginald, the very hopelessness of our love is a bond that binds us to one another!

Saphir: Jealousy is merged in misery. While he, the very cynosure of our eyes and hearts, remains icy insensible — what have we to strive for?

Ella: The love of maidens is, to him, as interesting as the taxes!

Saphir: Would that it were! He pays his taxes.

Angela: And cherishes the receipts! *(Enter Jane, L. U. E.)*

Saphir: Happy receipts! *(All sigh heavily.)*

Jane: *(L. C., suddenly)* Fools! *(They start, and turn to her.)*

Angela: I beg your pardon?

Jane: Fools and blind! The man loves — wildly loves!

Angela: But whom? None of us!

Jane: No, none of us. His weird fancy has lighted, for the nonce, on Patience, the village milkmaid!

Saphir: On Patience? Oh, it cannot be!

Jane: Bah! But yesterday I caught him in her dairy, eating fresh butter with a tablespoon. Today he is not well!

Saphir: But Patience boasts that she has never loved — that love is, to her, a sealed book! Oh, he cannot be serious!

Jane: 'Tis but a passing fancy — 'twill quickly wear away. *(aside, coming down-stage)* Oh, Reginald, if you but knew what a wealth of golden love is waiting for you, stored up in this rugged old bosom of mine, the milkmaid's triumph would be short indeed!

(Patience appears on the eminence, R. She looks down with pity on the despondent Ladies.)

No. 2. Still brooding on their mad infatuation!

Recitative

Patience, Saphir, Angela, and Chorus

hap - py girl! Loved by a po - et!
Patience
(going)
Your par - don, la - dies. I in - trude up - on you!
Angela
Nay, pret - ty child, come
(Patience descends.)
hith - er. Is it true that you have nev - er loved?
Patience
Most true in - deed.
Chorus
SOPRANO
Most mar - vel - ous!
ALTO
And most de - plor - a - ble!
Attacca

I cannot tell what this love may be

Solo

Patience

Allegretto grazioso ♩. = 76
Patience (L.C.)
p
1. I can - not tell what this love may
2. If love is a thorn, they show no
be That com-eth to all but not to me. It can-not be kind as they'd im -
wit Who fool-ish-ly hug and fos - ter it. If love is a weed, how sim - ple
ply, Or why do these la - dies sigh? It can-not be joy and rap - ture
they Who gath-er it day by day! If love is a net-tle that makes you

deep, Or why do these gen - tle la - dies weep? It can-not be bliss - ful as 'tis
smart, Then why do you wear it next your heart? And if it be none of these, Say
A
C
riten.
said, Or why are their eyes so — won-drous red?
I, — Ah, why do you sit and — sob and sigh?
a tempo
riten.
Though ev - 'ry - where true love I see
rall.
A-com-ing to all, — but not to me, I can-not tell what this love — may
rall.

B
D
a tempo
be! For I am blithe and I am gay, While they sit
a tempo
sigh-ing night and day, For I am blithe and I am gay, Think of the
Chorus
f
Yes, she is blithe and she is gay,
gulf 'twixt them and me, Think of the gulf 'twixt them and me, Fal la la la
p
Yes, she is blithe and gay, Yes, she is blithe and gay.

2d time ad lib.
la la la la la la la la la la la la la la la la la la la la la la la la la la la, and mis - er - ie!
Ah, mis - er - ie!
(She
dances across R. and back to R. C.)
f
1.
2.
p

Angela: Ah, Patience, if you have never loved, you have never known true happiness! *(All sigh.)*

Patience: *(C.)* But the truly happy alway seem to have so much on their minds. The truly happy never seem quite well.

Jane: *(coming L.C.)* There is a transcendentality of delirium — an acute accentuation of supremest ecstasy — which the earthy might easily mistake for indigestion. But it is *not* indigestion — it is æsthetic transfiguration! *(to the others)* Enough of babble. Come!

Patience: *(stopping her as she turns to go up C.)* But stay, I have some news for you. The 35th Dragoon Guards have halted in the village, and are even now on their way to this very spot.

Angela: The 35th Dragoon Guards!

Saphir: They are fleshly men, of full habit!

Ella: We care nothing for Dragoon Guards!

Patience: But, bless me, you were all engaged to them a year ago!

Saphir: A year ago!

Angela: My poor child, you don't understand these things. A year ago they were very well in our eyes, but since then our tastes have been etherealized, our preceptions exalted. *(to the others)* Come, it is time to lift up our voices in morning carol to our Reginald. Let us to his door!

(Angela leading, the Ladies go off, two and two, Jane last, over the drawbridge into the castle, singing refrain of "Twenty love-sick maidens", and, as before, accompanying themselves on harps, etc. Patience watches them in surprise, and, with a gesture of complete bafflement, climbs the rock and goes off the way she entered.)

No. 2a. Twenty love-sick maidens we

Chorus

Maidens

(The Officers of the Dragoon Guards enter, R., led by the Major. They form their line across the front of the stage.)

No. 3. The soldiers of our Queen

Chorus and Solo

Dragoons and Colonel

A
Chorus
TENOR f
The sol-diers of our Queen Are linked in friend-ly
BASS f
The sol-diers of our Queen Are linked in friend-ly
teth-er; Up-on the bat-tle scene They fight the foe to-geth-er. There
teth-er; Up-on the bat-tle scene They fight the foe to-geth-er. There
B
ev-'ry moth-er's son_ Pre-pared to fight and fall is; The en-e-my of
ev-'ry moth-er's son_ Pre-pared to fight and fall is; The en-e-my of

one The en e-my of all is! The en-e-my of one The
one The en-e-my of all is! The en-e-my of one The
(On an order from the Major they fall back.)
en-e-my of all is!
en-e-my of all is!
ff
(Enter the Colonel. All salute.)
Allegro ♩. = 108
ff

C
Colonel (C.)
If you want a re-ceipt for that
pop - u - lar mys - ter - y, Known to the world as a Heav - y Dra - goon,
Take
Chorus of Dragoons (saluting)
Yes, yes, yes, yes, yes, yes, yes!

all the re-mark-a-ble peo-ple in his-to-ry, Rat-tle them off to a
p
pop-u-lar tune.
D
f
Yes, yes, yes, yes,
f
yes, yes, yes!
The
fz
fz
p
3

pluck of Lord Nel-son on board of the Vic-to-ry— Ge-nius of Bis-mark de-
want a re-ceipt for this sol-dier-like par-a-gon, Get at the wealth of the
vis-ing a plan— The hu-mour of Field-ing (which sounds con-tra-dic-to-ry)—
Czar (if you can)— The fam-i-ly pride of a Span-iard from Ar-a-gon—
E
Cool-ness of Pa-get a-bout to tre-pan— The sci-ence of Jul-lien, the
Force of Me-phis-to pro-nounc-ing a ban— A smack of Lord Wa-ter-ford,
em-i-nent mu-si-co— Wit of Ma-cau-lay, who wrote of Queen Anne— The
reck-less and rol-lick-y— Swag-ger of Rod-er-ick, head-ing his clan— The

pa - thos of Pad - dy, as ren-dered by Bou - ci - cault— Style of the Bish - op of
keen pen - e - tra - tion of Pad-ding - ton Pol - la - ky — Grace of an O - da - lisque
So - dor and Man —The dash of a D'Or - say, di - vest - ed of quack - er - y —
on a di - van — The ge - nius stra - te - gic of Cæ - sar or Ha - ni - bal —
F
Nar - ra - tive pow - ers of Dick - ens and Thack - er - ay — Vic - tor Em - man - u - el —
Skill of Sir Gar - net in thrash - ing a can - ni - bal — Fla - vour of Ham - let—the
peak - haunt - ing Pe - ve - ril — Thom - as A - qui - nas and Doc - tor Sa - che - ve - rell —
Strang - er, a touch of him — Lit - tle of Man - fred (but not ver - y much of him) —

Tup-per and Ten-ny-son— Dan-iel De-foe— An-tho-ny Trol-lope and
Bea-dle of Bur-ling-ton— Ri-chard-son's show— Mis-ter Mi-caw-ber and
cre - - scen - do
Mis-ter Gui-zot!
Ma-dame Tus-saud!
Ah!
Chorus
TENOR
BASS
Yes, yes, yes, yes, yes, yes, yes, yes! A
G
Take of these el-e-ments all that is fu-si-ble, Melt 'em all down in a
Heav-y Dra-goon, a Heav-y Dra-goon, a Heav-y Dra-goon, a

pip-kin or cru-ci-ble— Set 'em to sim-mer and take off the scum,
Heav-y Dra-goon, a Heav-y Dra-goon, a Heav-y Dra-goon
2nd time
And a Heav - y Dra-goon is the re - si - du - um!
is the re - si - du - um!
f
ff
1.
2.
2. If you
ffz
(All "stand at ease.")

Colonel: Well, here we are once more on the scene of our former triumphs. But where's the Duke?

(Enter Duke, listlessly, and in low spirits, R.)

Duke: Here I am! *(Sighs.)*

Colonel: Come, cheer up, don't give way!

Duke: Oh, for that, I'm as cheerful as a poor devil can be expected to be who has the misfortune to be a Duke, with a thousand a day!

Major: Humph! Most men would envy you!

Duke: Envy *me*? Tell me, Major, are you fond of toffee?

Major: Very!

Colonel: We are all fond of toffee.

All: We are!

Duke: Yes, and toffee in moderation is a capital thing. But to *live* on toffee— toffee for breakfast, toffee for dinner, toffee for tea—to have it supposed that you care for nothing *but* toffee, and that you would consider yourself insulted if anything but toffee were offered to you— how would you like *that*?

Colonel: I can quite believe that, under those circumstances, even toffee would become monotonous.

Duke: For "toffee" read flattery, adulation, and abject deference, carried to such a pitch that I began, at last, to think that man was born bent at an angle of forty-five degrees! Great heavens, what is there to adulate in me? Am I particularly intelligent, or remarkably studious, or excruciatingly witty, or unusually accomplished, or exceptionally virtuous?

Colonel: You're about as commonplace a young man as ever I saw.

All: You are!

Duke: Exactly! That's it exactly! That describes me to a T! Thank you all very much! *(Shakes hands with the Colonel.)* Well, I couldn't stand it any longer, so I joined this second class cavalry regiment. In the army, thought I, I shall be occasionally snubbed, perhaps even bullied, who knows? The thought was rapture, and here I am.

Colonel: *(looking off)* Yes, and here are the ladies.

Duke: But who is the gentleman with the long hair?

Colonel: I don't know.

Duke: He seems popular!

Colonel: He *does* seem popular!

(The Dragoons back up R., watching the entrance of the Ladies. Bunthorne enters, L.U.E., followed by the Ladies, two and two, playing on harps as before. He is composing a poem, and is quite absorbed. He sees no one, but walks across the stage, followed by the Ladies, who take no notice of the Dragoons — to the surprise and indignation of those officers.)

No.4. In a doleful train

Chorus and Solos

Maidens, Ella, Angela, Saphir, Dragoons, and Bunthorne

(Bunthorne, the Ladies following, comes slowly down L. and then crosses the stage to R.)

Allegretto amoroso 𝅗𝅥=80

p
cresc.
f
dim.
Ella with SOPRANO
Angela & Saphir with ALTO
In a dole - ful
p
train Two and two we walk all day, For we love in

vain! None so sor-row-ful as they Who__ can on - ly
sigh and say, Woe is me, a - lack - a -
day!__ Woe is me, a - lack - a - day!
A
Chorus of Dragoons
f
Now
mf
is not this ri - dic - u - lous, and is not this pre - pos - ter - ous? A

thor-ough-paced ab-surd-i-ty— ex-plain it if you can. In-
stead of rush-ing ea-ger-ly to cher-ish us and fos-ter us, They
all pre-fer this me-lan-chol-y lit-er-a-ry man. In-
B
stead of sly-ly peer-ing at us, Cast-ing looks en-dear-ing at us,

Blush-ing at us, flush-ing at us, flirt-ing with a fan; They're
ac-tu-al-ly sneer-ing at us, fleer-ing at us, jeer-ing at us!
Pret-ty sort of treat-ment for a mil-i-ta-ry man! They're
ac-tu-al-ly sneer-ing at us, fleer-ing at us, jeer-ing at us!

Pret-ty sort of treat-ment for a mil-i-ta-ry man!
(Bunthorne, C.)
dim.
rall.
Andantino ♩= 84
1st time: Angela (R. of Bunthorne)
2nd time: Saphir (L. of Bunthorne)
Mys-tic po-et, hear our prayer,
Though so ex-cel-lent-ly wise,
Twen-ty love-sick maid-ens
For a mo-ment mor-tal
p
we—
be,
Young and weal-thy, dark and fair,
Deign to raise thy pur-ple eyes
All of coun-ty
From thy heart-drawn

D
G
fam - i - ly.
po - e - sy.
And we die for love of thee –
Twen - ty love-sick maidens see –
Twen - ty love-sick maid-ens we!
Each is kneel-ing on her knee!
Maidens (2nd time, kneeling)
Yes, we die for love of thee –
Twen-ty love-sick maid-ens see –
Twen - ty love-sick maid-ens we!
Each is kneel-ing on her knee!
dim.
E
Bunthorne (1st time, crossing to L.)
(2nd time, going R.)
Though my
Though as
Allegro come I° (𝅗𝅥 = 80)
book I seem to scan In a rapt ec - sta - tic way, Like a
I re-marked be - fore, An - y - one convinced would be That some
p stac.

lit - er - a - ry man Who de - spi - ses fe - male clay; I hear
tran - scen - den - tal lore Is mo - no - po - liz - ing me, 'Round the
F
H
(1st time, Bunthorne crosses to C.)
f Dragoons
plain - ly all they say, Twen - ty love - sick maid - ens they! He hears plain - ly all they
cor - ner I can see Each is kneel - ing on her knee! 'Round the cor - ner he can
1. Andantino (♩ = 84)
2.
say, Twen - ty love - sick maid - ens they!
see Each is kneel - ing on her knee! Now is not this ri -
dic - u - lous, and is not this pre - pos - ter - ous? A thor - ough - paced ab -

J
surd-i-ty– ri-dic-u-lous! pre - pos-ter-ous! Ex-plain it if you can.
sf
sf
Maidens
f
In a dole - ful train Two and
Dragoons f
Now is not this ri-dic-u-lous, and is not this pre-pos-ter-ous? A
f
two we walk all day, For we
thor-ough-paced ab-surd-i-ty– ex - plain it if you can. In -

love in vain! None so
stead of rush-ing ea-ger-ly to cher-ish us and fos-ter us, They
sor-row-ful as they
all pre-fer this me-lan-chol-y lit-er-a-ry man. In-
Who can on-ly
stead of sly-ly peer-ing at us, Cast-ing looks en-dear-ing at us,

sigh and say,
Blush-ing at us, flush-ing at us, flirt-ing with a fan; They're
K
Woe is me, a -
ac - tu - al - ly sneer-ing at us, fleer-ing at us, jeer-ing at us!
lack - a - day!
Pret - ty sort of treat-ment for a mil - i - ta - ry man! They're

Woe is me, a -
ac - tu - al - ly sneer - ing at us, fleer - ing at us, jeer - ing at us!
ff
lack - a - day! Twen - ty
Pret - ty sort of treat - ment for a mil - i - ta - ry man! Now
ff
L
love - sick maid - ens
is not this ri - dic - u - lous, and is not this pre - pos - ter - ous? They

we, And we
all pre - fer this me - lan - chol - y lit - er - a - ry man. Now
die for love of
is not this ri - dic - u - lous, and is not this pre - pos - ter - ous? They
thee! Yes, we
all pre - fer this me - lan - chol - y, me - lan - chol - y lit - er - a - ry

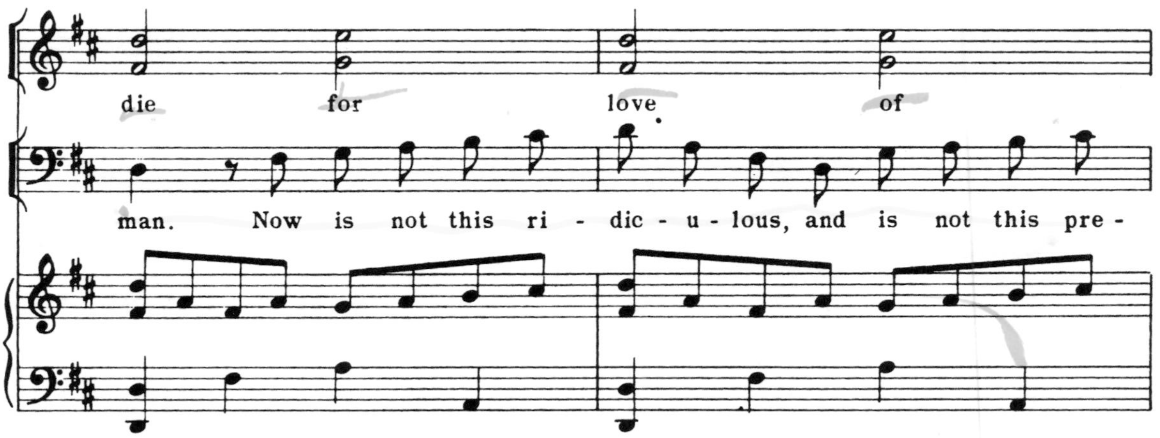

Colonel: *(R.C.)* Angela! What is the meaning of this?

Angela: *(C.)* Oh, sir, leave us; our minds are but ill-tuned to light love-talk.

Major: *(L.C.)* But what in the world has come over you all?

Jane: *(L.C.)* Bunthorne. *He* has come over us. He has come among us, and he has idealized us.

Duke: Has he succeeded in idealizing *you*?

Jane: He has!

Duke: Good old Bunthorne!

Jane: My eyes are open; I droop despairingly; I am soulfully intense; I am limp and I cling!

(During this, Bunthorne is seen in all the agonies of composition. The Ladies are watching him intently as he writhes. At last he hits on the word he wants and writes it down. A general sigh of relief.)

Bunthorne: Finished! At last! Finished! *(He staggers, overcome with mental strain, into the arms of the Colonel.)*

Colonel: Are you better now?

Bunthorne: Yes — oh, it's you! — I am better now. The poem is finished, and my soul has gone out into it. That was all. It was nothing worth mentioning, it occurs three times a day. *(Sees Patience, who has entered during this scene.)* Ah, Patience! Dear Patience! *(Holds her hand; she seems frightened.)*

Angela: Will it please you read it to us, sir?

Saphir: This we supplicate. *(All kneel.)*

Bunthorne: Shall I?

All the Dragoons: No!

Bunthorne: *(annoyed—to Patience)* I will read it if *you* bid me!

Patience: *(much frightened)* You can if you like!

Bunthorne: It is a wild, weird, fleshly thing; yet very tender, very yearning, very precious. It is called, "Oh, Hollow! Hollow! Hollow!"

Patience: Is it a hunting song?

Bunthorne: A hunting song? No, it is *not* a hunting song. It is the wail of the poet's heart on discovering that everything is commonplace. To understand it, cling passionately to one another and think of faint lilies. *(They do so as he recites.)*

"Oh, Hollow! Hollow! Hollow!"

What time the poet hath hymned
The writhing maid, lithe-limbed,
  Quivering on amaranthine asphodel,
How can he paint her woes,
Knowing, as well he knows,
  That all can be set right with calomel?

When from the poet's plinth
The amorous colocynth
  Yearns for the aloe, faint with rapturous thrills,
How can he hymn their throes,
Knowing, as well he knows,
  That they are only uncompounded pills?

Is it, and can it be,
Nature hath this decree,
  Nothing poetic in the world shall dwell?
Or that in all her works
Something poetic lurks,
  Even in colocynth and calomel?
      I cannot tell!

(He goes off, L.U.E. All turn and watch him, not speaking until he has gone.)

Angela: How purely fragrant!

Saphir: How earnestly precious!

Patience: Well, it seems to me to be nonsense.

Saphir: Nonsense, yes, perhaps,—but oh, what precious nonsense!

Colonel: This is all very well, but you seem to forget that you are engaged to us.

Saphir: It can never be. You are not Empyrean. You are not Della Cruscan. You are not even Early English. Oh, be Early English ere it is too late! *(Officers look at each other in astonishment.)*

Jane: *(looking at uniform)* Red and yellow! Primary colors! Oh, South Kensington!

Duke: We didn't design our uniforms, but we don't see how they could be improved!

Jane: No, you wouldn't. Still, there *is* a oobwebby grey velvet, with a tender bloom like cold gravy, which, made Florentine fourteenth century, trimmed with Venetian leather and Spanish altar lace, and surmounted with something Japanese—it matters not what—would at least be Early English! Come, maidens.

(Exit Maidens, L.U.E., two and two, singing refrain of "Twenty lovesick maidens we". Patience goes off L. The Officers watch the Ladies go off in astonishment.)

No. 4a. Twenty love-sick maidens we

Chorus

Maidens

Andantino ♩= 84
(As the Maidens depart, the Dragoons spread across the stage.)
Maidens
Twen - ty love-sick maid-ens we,
p dolce
Love-sick all a-gainst our will.
Twen - ty years hence
we shall be
Twen - ty love-sick maid-ens still.
8
Ah, mis - - er - ie!
smorz.

Duke: Gentlemen, this is an insult to the British uniform.

Colonel: A uniform that has been as successful in the courts of Venus as on the field of Mars!

No. 5. When I first put this uniform on

Solo and Chorus

Colonel and Dragoons

(The Dragoons form their original line.)
Allegro marziale ♩=108
ff
Colonel
1. When I first put this u-ni-form on, I said, as I looked in the glass, "It's one to a mil-lion That an-y ci-vil-ian My fig-ure and form will sur-pass. Gold
said, when I first put it on, "It is plain to the ver-i-est dunce, That ev-e-ry beau-ty Will feel it her du-ty To yield to its glam-our at once. They will
p

lace has a charm for the fair, And I've plen - ty of that, and to
see that I'm free - ly gold-laced In a u - ni-form hand-some and
spare, While a lov - er's pro-fes - sions, When ut - tered in Hes - sians, Are
chaste"— But the per - i - pa-tet - ics Of long-haired æs-thet - ics Are
e - lo-quent ev - 'ry - where!" A — fact that I count - ed up -
ver - y much more to their taste— Which I nev - er count - ed up -
on, When I first put this un - i - form on!
on, When I first put this un - i - form on!
Chorus of Dragoons
f
By a
By a

sim - ple co - in - ci - dence, few Could ev - er have count - ed up - on, The
I
sim - ple co - in - ci - dence, few Could ev - er have count - ed up - on, The
I
same thing oc - curred to me, When I first put this u - ni - form
did - n't an - ti - ci - pate that,
same thing oc - curred to me, When I first put this u - ni - form
did - n't an - ti - ci - pate that,
1. Colonel
2.
(The Dragoons go off angrily, R.)
on! 2. I on!
on! on!
ff

(Enter Bunthorne, L.U.E., who changes his manner and becomes intensely melodramatic.)

No. 6. Am I alone and unobserved?

Recitative and Solo

Bunthorne

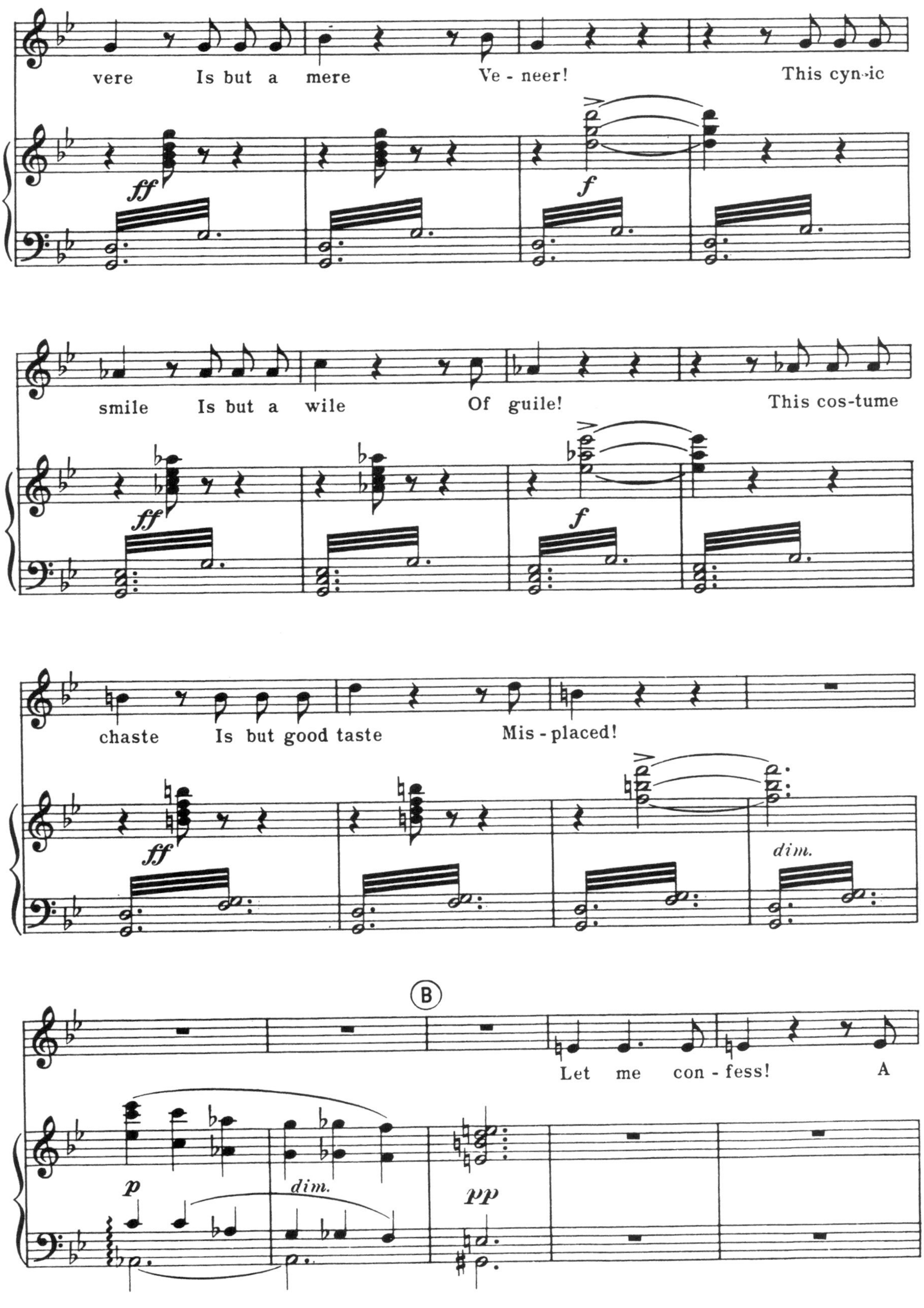
vere Is but a mere Ve - neer! This cyn-ic
ff
f
smile Is but a wile Of guile! This cos-tume
ff
f
chaste Is but good taste Mis - placed!
ff
dim.
B
Let me con - fess! A
p
dim.
pp

Recit.
languid love for lilies does not blight me! Lank limbs and haggard cheeks do not delight me! I do
p
con pedale
not care for dirty greens By any means. I do not long for all one sees That's Japanese.— I am
not fond of uttering platitudes In stained-glass attitudes. In short, my
me-di-æ-val-is-m's af-fec-ta-tion, Born of a mor-bid love of ad-mi-ra-tion!

(Tiptoes up-stage, looking L. and R., and comes back down, C.)

Allegretto grazioso ♩ = 76
p
1. If you're anx-ious for to shine_ in the
el - o-quent in praise of the
sen - ti - men-tal pas-sion of a
p stacc.
high æs-thet-ic line_ as a man of cul - ture rare, You must
ver - y dull old days_ which have long since passed a - way, And con -
veg - e - ta - ble fash-ion must ex - cite your lan-guid spleen, An at -

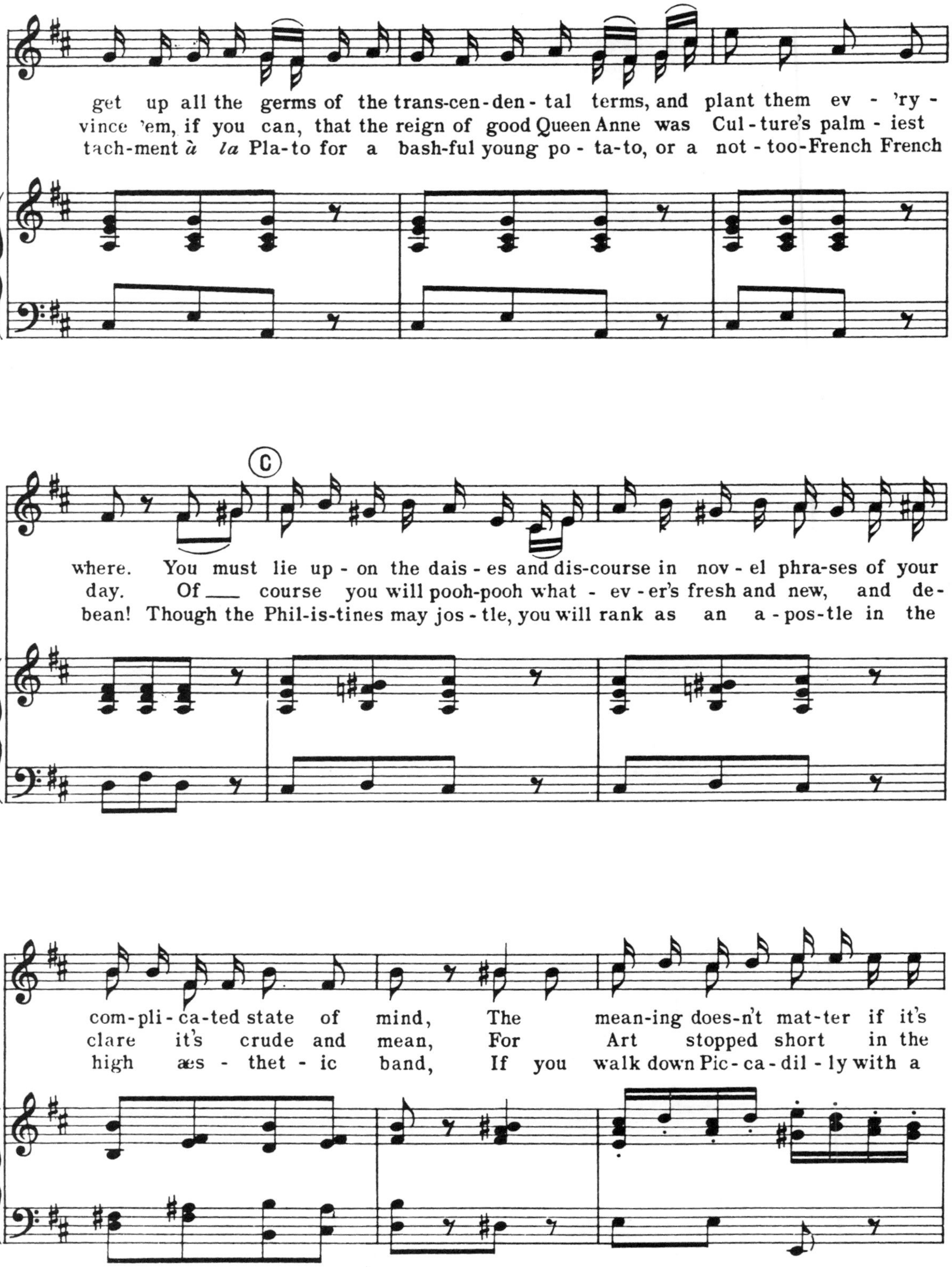
get up all the germs of the trans-cen-den - tal terms, and plant them ev - 'ry -
vince 'em, if you can, that the reign of good Queen Anne was Cul - ture's palm - iest
tach-ment à la Pla-to for a bash-ful young po - ta-to, or a not - too-French French
C
where. You must lie up - on the dais - es and dis-course in nov - el phra-ses of your
day. Of ___ course you will pooh-pooh what - ev - er's fresh and new, and de-
bean! Though the Phil-is-tines may jos - tle, you will rank as an a - pos-tle in the
com-pli - ca-ted state of mind, The mean-ing does-n't mat-ter if it's
clare it's crude and mean, For Art stopped short in the
high æs - thet - ic band, If you walk down Pic - ca - dil - ly with a

on-ly i-dle chat-ter of a trans-cen-den-tal kind.
cul-ti-va-ted court of the Em-press Jo-seph-ine.
pop-py or a lil-y in your me-di-æ-val hand.
D
And ev-'ry-one will say, As you walk your mys-tic
And ev-'ry-one will say, As you walk your mys-tic
And ev-'ry-one will say, As you walk your flow-'ry
pp sempre stacc.
way, "If this young man ex-press-es him-self in
way, "If that's not good e-nough for him which is
way, "If he's con-tent with a veg-e-ta-ble love which would

E
terms too deep for me, Why, what a ver-y sin-gu-lar-ly
good e-nough for me, Why, what a ver-y cul-ti-va-ted
cer-tain-ly not suit me, Why, what a most par-tic-u-lar-ly
last verse rall.
deep young man this deep young man must be!"
kind of youth this kind of youth must be!"
pure young man this pure young man must be!"
tr
last verse rall.
1.2.
3.
2. Be
3. Then a

(At the end of the song, Patience enters, L. He sees her.)

Bunthorne: Ah! Patience, come hither. *(She comes to him, timidly.)* I am pleased with thee. The bitter-hearted one, who finds all else hollow, is pleased with thee. For *you* are not hollow. *Are* you?

Patience: No, thanks, I have dined; but—I beg your pardon—I interrupt you. *(Turns to go; he stops her.)*

Bunthorne: Life is made up of interruptions. The tortured soul, yearning for solitude, writhes under them. Oh, but my heart is a-weary! Oh, I am a cursed thing! *(She attempts to escape.)* Don't go!

Patience: Really, I'm very sorry.

Bunthorne: Tell me, girl, do you ever yearn?

Patience: I earn my living.

Bunthorne: *(impatiently)* No, No! Do you know what it is to be heart-hungry? Do you know what it is to yearn for the Indefinable, and yet to be brought face to face, daily, with the Multiplication Table? Do you know what it is to seek oceans and to find puddles? That's my case. Oh, I am a cursed thing! *(She turns again.)* Don't go.

Patience: If you please, I don't understand you—you frighten me!

Bunthorne: Don't be frightened—it's only poetry.

Patience: Well, if that's poetry, I don't like poetry.

Bunthorne: *(eagerly)* Don't you? *(aside)* Can I trust her? *(aloud)* Patience, you don't like poetry—well, between you and me, *I* don't like poetry. It's hollow, unsubstantial—unsatisfactory. What's the use of yearning for Elysian Fields when you know you can't get 'em, and would only let 'em out on building leases if you had 'em?

Patience: Sir, I—

Bunthorne: Patience, I have long loved you. Let me tell you a secret. I am not as bilious as I look. If you like, I will cut my hair. There is more innocent fun within me than a casual spectator would imagine. You have never seen me frolicsome. Be a good girl—a very good girl—and one day you shall. If you are fond of touch-and-go jocularity—this is the shop for it.

Patience: Sir, I will speak plainly. In the matter of love I am untaught. I have never loved but my great-aunt. But I am quite certain that, under any circumstances, I couldn't possibly love *you*.

Bunthorne: Oh, you think not?

Patience: I'm quite sure of it. Quite sure. Quite.

Bunthorne: Very good. Life is henceforth a blank. I don't care what becomes of me. I have only to ask that you will not abuse my confidence; though *you* despise me, I am extremely popular with the other young ladies.

Patience: I only ask that you leave me and never renew the subject.

Bunthorne: Certainly. Broken-hearted and desolate, I go. *(Goes up-stage, suddenly turns and recites.)*

"Oh, to be wafted away,
From this black Aceldama of sorrow,
Where the dust of an earthy today
Is the earth of a dusty tomorrow!"

It is a little thing of my own. I call it "Heart Foam". I shall not publish it. Farewell! Patience, Patience, farewell! *(Exit Bunthorne.)*

Patience: What on earth does it all mean? Why does he love me? Why does he expect me to love him? *(going R.)* He's not a relation! It frightens me!

(Enter Angela, L.)

Angela: Why, Patience, what is the matter?

Patience: Lady Angela, tell me two things. Firstly, what on earth is this love that upsets everybody; and, secondly, how is it to be distinguished from insanity?

Angela: Poor blind child! Oh, forgive her, Eros! Why, love is of all passions the most essential! It is the embodiment of purity, the abstraction of refinement! It is the one unselfish emotion in this whirlpool of grasping greed!

Patience: Oh, dear, oh! *(beginning to cry.)*

Angela: Why are you crying?

Patience: To think that I have lived all these years without having experienced this ennobling and unselfish passion! Why, what a wicked girl I must be! For it *is* unselfish, isn't it?

Angela: Absolutely! Love that is tainted with selfishness is no love! Oh, try, try, try to love! It really isn't difficult if you give your whole mind to it.

Patience: I'll set about it at once. I won't go to bed until I'm head over ears in love with somebody.

Angela: Noble girl! But is it possible that you have never loved anybody?

Patience: Yes, one.

Angela: Ah! Whom?

Patience: My great-aunt—

Angela: Great-aunts don't count.

Patience: Then there's nobody. At least—no, nobody. Not since I was a baby. But *that* doesn't count, I suppose.

Angela: I don't know. Tell me all about it.

No. 7. Long years ago, fourteen maybe

Duet

Patience and Angela

Allegretto moderato ♩ = 108
Patience (R.)
Long years a - go,
four-teen, may-be, When but a ti-ny babe of four, An-
oth - er ba - by played with me, My el-der by a year or
more. A lit-tle child of beauty rare, With mar-v'lous eyes and won-drous hair,
p
p
cresc.
A

Who, in my child-eyes, seemed to me All that a lit-tle child should be!
p
mf
(She goes to Angela, L.C.)
B
Ah, how we loved, that
dim.
p
child and I, How pure our ba-by joy! How true our love—
and, by the bye, He was a lit-tle boy!
Angela
Ah,

C
old, old tale of Cu-pid's touch! I thought as much— I
p
stacc.
Patience
Pray
thought as much! He was a lit-tle boy!
p
don't mis-con-strue what I say— Re-mem-ber, pray— re-
p
stacc.
D
mem-ber, pray, He was a lit-tle boy!
No doubt! Yet, spite of all your pains, The
f

Patience: *(R. C.)* It's perfectly dreadful to think of the appalling state I must be in! I had no idea that love was a duty. No wonder they all look so unhappy! Upon my word, I hardly like to associate with myself. I don't think I'm respectable. I'll go at once and fall in love with. . . *(As she turns to go up R., Grosvenor enters, R.U.E. She sees him and turns back.)* a stranger!

No. 8. Prithee, pretty maiden

Duet

Patience and Grosvenor

(coming down-stage)
wa - ly O! I would fain dis-cov - er If you have a lov - er!
wa - ly O! Mon-ey, I de-spise it, Man-y peo-ple prize it,
rall.
Patience (L.)
a tempo
Hey___ wil - low wa - ly___ O! Gen-tle sir, my heart is
Hey___ wil - low wa - ly___ O! Gen-tle sir, al-though to
rall.
a tempo
frol-ic-some and free— (Hey, but he's dole-ful, wil-low wil-low wa - ly!)
mar-ry I de-sign— (Hey, but he's hope-ful, wil-low wil-low wa - ly!) As

Nobody I care for comes a-courting me— Hey willow
yet I do not know you, and so I must decline— Hey willow
wa - ly O! Nobody I care for Comes a-courting—therefore,
wa - ly O! To other maidens go you— As yet I do not know you,
1. rall.
2. rall.
Hey wil - low wa - ly O!
Hey wil - low wa - ly O'
Grosvenor rall.
Hey wil-low wa - ly O!
rall.
rall.

Grosvenor: Patience! Can it be that you don't recognize me?

Patience: *(down L.)* Recognize you? No, indeed I don't!

Grosvenor: Have fifteen years so greatly changed me?

Patience: *(turning to him)* Fifteen years? What do you mean?

Grosvenor: Have you forgotten the friend of your youth, your Archibald?—your little playfellow? Oh, Chronos, Chronos, this is too bad of you! *(Comes down, C.)*

Patience: Archibald! Is it possible? Why, let me look! It is! It is! *(Takes his hands.)* It must be! Oh, how happy I am! I thought we should never meet again! And how you've grown!

Grosvenor: Yes, Patience, I am much taller and much stouter than I was.

Patience: And how you've improved!

Grosvenor: *(dropping her hands and turning)* Yes, Patience, I am very beautiful! *(Sighs.)*

Patience: But surely that doesn't make you unhappy?

Grosvenor: Yes, Patience. Gifted as I am with a beauty which probably has not its rival on earth, I am, nevertheless, utterly and completely miserable.

Patience: Oh, but why?

Grosvenor: My child-love for you has never faded. Conceive, then, the horror of my situation when I tell you that it is my hideous destiny to be madly loved at first sight by every woman I come across!

Patience: But why do you make yourself so picturesque? Why not disguise yourself, disfigure yourself, anything to escape this persecution?

Grosvenor: No, Patience, that may not be. These gifts—irksome as they are—were given to me for the enjoyment and delectation of my fellow-creatures. I am a trustee for Beauty, and it is my duty to see that the conditions of my trust are faithfully discharged.

Patience: And you, too, are a Poet?

Grosvenor: Yes, I am the Apostle of Simplicity. I am called "Archibald the All-Right"—for I am infallible.

Patience: And is it possible that you condescend to love such a girl as I?

Grosvenor: Yes, Patience, is it not strange? I have loved you with a Florentine fourteenth century frenzy for a full fifteen years.

Patience: Oh, marvelous! I have hitherto been deaf to the voice of love. I seem now to know what love is! It has been revealed to me—it is Archibald Grosvenor!

Grosvenor: Yes, Patience, it is! *(She goes into his arms.)*

Patience: *(as in a trance)* We will never, never part!

Grosvenor: We will live and die together!

Patience: I swear it!

Grosvenor: We both swear it!

Patience: *(recoiling from him)* But—oh, horror!

Grosvenor: What's the matter?

Patience: Why, you are perfection! A source of endless ecstasy to all who know you!

Grosvenor: I know I am. Well?

Patience: Then, bless my heart, there can be nothing unselfish in loving *you!*

Grosvenor: Merciful powers! I never thought of that!

Patience: To monopolize those features on which all women love to linger! It would be unpardonable!

Grosvenor: Why, so it would! Oh, fatal perfection, again you interpose between me and my happiness!

Patience: Oh, if you were but a thought less beautiful than you are!

Grosvenor: Would that I were! but candour compels me to admit that I'm not!

Patience: Our duty is clear; we must part, and for ever!

Grosvenor: Oh, misery! And yet I cannot question the propriety of your decision. Farewell, Patience!

Patience: Farewell, Archibald! *(They both turn to go.)*

Patience: *(suddenly)* But stay!

Grosvenor: Yes, Patience?

Patience: Although I may not love *you*—for you are perfection—there is nothing to prevent your loving *me.* I am plain, homely, unattractive!

Grosvenor: Why, that's true!

Patience: The love of such a man as you for such a girl as I must be unselfish!

Grosvenor: Unselfishness itself!

No. 8a. Though to marry you would very selfish be

Duet

Patience and Grosvenor

Allegretto
Patience
Though to mar - ry you would ver - y self-ish be—
Grosvenor
(Hey, but I'm dole-ful, wil-low wil-low wa - ly!)
You may all the same con - tin-ue lov-ing me.
(Hey, wil-low wa - ly O!)
All the world ig-nor-ing,
All the world ig-nor-ing,
You'll go on a - dor - ing, Hey, wil - low wa - ly O!
I'll go on a - dor - ing, Hey, wil - low wa - ly O!
p

(They go off sadly—Patience, L., Grosvenor, R. U. E.)

No. 9. Let the merry cymbals sound

Finale of Act I

Ensemble

(Enter Bunthorne, crowned with roses and hung about with garlands and looking very miserable. He is led by Angela and Saphir (each of whom holds an end of the rose-garland by which he is bound), and accompanied by procession of Maidens. They are dancing classically, and playing on cymbals, double pipes, and other archaic instruments. Jane last, with a very large pair of cymbals.)

(The procession enters over the drawbridge, Bunthorne being preceded by the Chorus.

They go R. and round the stage, ending with Bunthorne down L. C., with Angela on his

R., Saphir on his L., Jane up C.)

A
Chorus of Maidens
Let the mer-ry cym-bals sound,
Gai - ly pipe Pan-dæ - an
cresc.
pleas - ure,
With a Daph-ne-phor-ic bound

Tread a gay but clas - sic meas - - ure, Tread a gay but clas - sic
meas - ure.
B
Ev - 'ry heart with hope is
beat - ing, For, at this ex - cit - ing meet - ing,
Fick - le For - tune will de - cide Who shall be our Bun - thorne's bride!

Ev - 'ry heart with hope is beat - ing,
For, at this ex-cit - ing meet - ing, Fick - le For-tune will de -
C
cide Who shall be our Bun - thorne's bride! Let the mer - ry cym-bals
ff
sound, — Gai - ly pipe Pan-dæ - an pleas - ure,

With a Daph-ne-phor-ic bound
Tread a gay but clas-sic,
clas-sic meas-ure, Tread a gay but clas-sic, clas-sic meas-ure, A
clas-sic meas-ure.
(Dragoons enter down R., forming
D
Allegro alla Marcia ♩= 108
f
p
line diagonally up to up-stage, C.)
Duke, Col., & Maj., Cho. of Dragoons
TENOR & BASS Unis. f
Now
cresc.

tell us, we pray you, Why thus they ar-ray you— Oh, po - et, how say you—What
mf
is it you've done? Now tell us, we pray you, Why thus they ar-ray you— Oh,
po - et, how say you—What is it you've done? Oh, po - et, how say you—What
E
Duke (C.)
is it you've done? Of rite sa-cri - fi - cial, By sen-tence ju - di - cial, This
p

Colonel (R. C.)
seems the in - i - tial, Then why don't you run? They can - not have led you To
hang or be - head you, Nor may they all wed you, Un - for - tu-nate one! Then
Chorus
fz
tell us, we pray you, Why thus they ar-ray you— Oh po - et, how say you— What
mf
F
Recit. Bunthorne
is it you've done? Heart-bro-ken at my Pa-tien-ce's bar-bar-i - ty,
p

By the ad-vice of my so - lic - i - tor, In aid— in aid of
(He introduces his solicitor.)
a de-serv-ing char-i - ty, I've put my-self up to be raf - fled for!
G
Chorus of Maidens
By the ad-vice of his so - lic - i - tor, He's put him-self up to be
p a tempo
Chorus of Dragoons
raf-fled for! Oh, hor-ror! urged by his so - lic - i - tor, He's

Chorus of Maidens
p
Oh, heav-en's bless-ing on
put him-self up to be raf-fled for!
his so-lic-i-tor!
f
A hid-eous curse on his so-lic-i-tor!
p
Oh,
p
heav-en's bless-ing on his so-lic-i-tor!
f
A hid-eous curse on

A bless-ing on his so-
his so - lic - i-tor! A curse, a
p
pp
f
(The Solicitor, horrified at the Dragoons' curse, rushes off, L.)
rall.
lic - i - tor!
curse on his so - lic - i-tor!
Allegro ♩. = 108
Colonel (R.C.)
(Bunthorne up L., surrounded by the Ladies
Stay, we im-plore you, Be-fore our hopes are blight - ed; You see be-fore you The men to whom you're plight - ed!

Chorus
TENOR
Stay, we implore you, For we adore you; To
BASS
Stay, we implore you, For we adore you; To
us you're plighted To be united—
us you're plighted To be united—
cresc.
Stay, we implore, we implore you!
Stay, we implore, we implore you!
f

Andante con tenerezza ♩= 76
Duke (C.)
Your maid-en hearts, ah, do not steel To pit - y's el-o-quent ap - peal, Such con-duct Brit - ish sol-diers feel.
(aside)
Sigh, sigh, all sigh!
(They all sigh.)
To foe-man's steel we rare-ly see A Brit-ish sol-dier bend the knee,
Yet, one and all, they kneel to ye—
(aside)
Kneel, kneel, all
p
f
p

(They all kneel.)
kneel! Our sol-diers ver - y sel-dom cry, And yet— I need not tell you
f
p
why— A tear-drop dews each mar-tial eye! Weep, weep, all
(aside)
(They all weep.)
weep!
Chorus of Maidens
cresc.
Our sol-diers ver - y sel-dom cry, And yet—they need not tell us
Chorus of Dragoons
cresc.
We sol-diers ver - y sel-dom cry, And yet— we need not tell you
cresc.

A tear-drop dews each mar-tial eye! — Weep, weep, all weep!
(Bunthorne shows his impatience.)
p
why— Weep, weep, all weep!
p
why— A tear dews each eye! — Weep, weep, all weep!
p
pp
Allegro vivace 𝅗𝅥 = 92
Bunthorne (coming briskly forward, L. C.)
(The Solicitor re-enters.)
Come, walk up, and pur-chase with a-vid-i-ty,
p stacc.
O-ver-come your dif-fi-dence and nat-u-ral ti-mid-i-ty,
Tick-ets for the raf-fle should be pur-chased with a-vid-i-ty,

Put in half a guin - ea and a hus - band you may gain—
Such a judge of blue-and-white and oth - er kinds of pot - ter - y— From
ear - ly O - ri - en - tal down to mod - ern ter - ra - cot - ta - ry—
Put in half a guin - ea— you may draw him in a lot - ter - y—

Such an op - por - tu - ni - ty may not oc - cur a - gain.
K
Chorus of Maidens
Such a judge of blue-and-white and oth - er kinds of pot - te - ry— From
più f
ear - ly O - ri - en - tal down to mod - ern ter - ra - cot - ta - ry—
Put in half a guin - ea— you may draw him in a lot - ter - y—

Such an op - por - tu - ni - ty may not oc - cur a - gain.
(Maidens crowd up to purchase tickets.)
Vivace ♩. = 112
Chorus of Dragoons
(Dragoons dance in single file around
f TENOR & BASS
We've been thrown o - ver,
f
stage to express their indifference.)
we're a - ware, But we don't care— but we don't care! There's
fish in the sea, no doubt of it, As good as ev - er came

out of it,
And some day we shall
get our share,
So we don't care— so
we don't care!
M
(During this, the Girls have been buying tickets, the Solicitor
officiating.)

(At last Jane presents herself. Bunthorne looks at her with aversion.)
Recit. Bunthorne
Jane
And are you go-ing a tick-et for to buy? Most
p
(surprised)
Bunthorne (aside)
cer-tain-ly I am; why should-n't I? Oh, For-tune, this is hard!
a tempo moderato
(aloud)
Blind-fold your eyes; Two min-utes will de-cide who wins the
(Girls blindfold themselves.)
N
Andante affettuoso ♩= 76
Chorus of Maidens
prize! Oh, For-tune, to my ach-ing heart be
p

kind; Like us, thou art blind-fold-ed, but not
(Each uncovers one eye.)
blind! Just raise your band-age, thus, that you may
see, And give the prize, and give the prize to
O
(They cover their eyes again.)
me!
p

Bunthorne
Jane (joyfully)
Come, La-dy Jane, I pray you draw the first! He loves me
best!
Bunthorne (aside)
I want to know the worst!
Q
(Jane puts her hand in bag to draw ticket. Patience enters and prevents her.)
Allegro vivace ♩= 144
Recit. Patience (L. C.)
Hold! stay your hand!
ff
f a tempo
Chorus of Maidens
(uncovering their eyes)
f
What means this in - ter -
Chorus of Dragoons
f
What means this in - ter -

fer - ence? Of this bold girl I
fer - ence? Of this bold girl I
Jane
pray you make a clear - ance! A -
pray you make a clear - ance!
way with you, a - way with you, and to your milk - pails
Bunthorne (suddenly)
Patience
go! She wants a tick-et! Take a doz-en! No! If
p
cresc.
f

R
there be par - don in your breast For this poor pen - i - tent, Who
p
with re-morse-ful thought op-prest, Sin - cere - ly doth re - pent. If
you, with one so low - ly, still de - sire to be al -
ad lib.
lied, Then you may take me, if you will, For I will be your
colla voce

S
(She kneels to Bunthorne.)
bride!
ff
Chorus
ff
Oh, shame - less one! Oh, bold - faced thing! A - way you
Oh, shame - less one! Oh, bold - faced thing! A - way you
ff
run— Go, take your wing, Ah,
Oh, shame - less one! Oh, bold - faced
run— Go, take your wing, Ah,
thing! Go, take your wing, You shame - less
A - way you run— Go, take your wing, You shame - less

(Bunthorne raises her.)
Bunthorne
one! You bold - faced thing! How
one! You bold - faced thing!
p
T
strong is love! For many and many a week, She's
p
loved me fond - ly, and has feared to speak, But
Na - ture, for re-straint too might - y far, Has

U
ad lib. (spoken)
burst the bonds of Art—
And here we are!
f
f
Recit. Patience
No, Mis-ter Bun-thorne, no— you're wrong a - gain, Per - mit me— I'll en-
p
deav-our to ex - plain!
Clar. Solo
V
Andante ♩= 84
Patience
True love must sin-gle-heart-ed be—
From ev-'ry self-ish fan - cy
Bunthorne
Ex-act-ly so!
Andante ♩= 84
p

free—
No i-dle thought of gain or— joy A
Ex-act-ly so!
maid-en's fan-cy should em-ploy—
True love must be with-out al-
cresc.
loy, True love must be with-out al-loy.
W
Im-pos-ture to con-tempt must
Men
Ex-act-ly so!
p

lead— Blind van-i-ty's dis-sen-sion's seed— It
Colonel (R.C.)
Major (R.)
Ex-act-ly so—
Ex-act-ly so—
fol-lows, then, a maid-en— who De-votes her-self to
lov-ing— you Is prompt-ed— by no self-ish view, Is
cresc.
dim.

Y
Saphir (coming L. of Bunthorne)
prompt-ed by no self - ish view!
Are you re-solved to wed this
Men
Ex-act-ly so!
p
pp
Angela (coming R. of Bunthorne)
Bunthorne
shame-less one?
Is there no chance for an-y oth-er?
None!
(Exit Patience and Bunthorne, L. Angela, Saphir, and Ella take Colonel, Duke, and Major down, while Girls gaze fondly at other Officers.)
Andante con moto ♩ = 88
p

A
Ella
p
I
Saphir
p
I
Angela
p
I
Duke
p
I
Major
p
I
Colonel
p
I
A
p
hear the soft note of the ech - o-ing voice Of an old, old love, long
hear the soft note of the ech - o-ing voice Of an old, old love, long
hear the soft note of the ech - o - ing voice Of an old, old love, long
hear the soft note of the ech - o-ing voice Of an old, old love, long
hear the soft note of the ech - o-ing voice Of an old, old love, long
hear the soft note of the ech - o - ing voice Of an old, old love, long

cresc.
dead— It whis-pers my sor - row - ing heart "re - joice"— For the
cresc.
dead— It whis-pers my sor - row - ing heart "re - joice"— For the
cresc.
dead— It whis-pers my sor - row - ing heart "re - joice"— For the
cresc.
dead— It whis-pers my sor - row - ing heart "re - joice"— For the
cresc.
dead— It whis-pers my sor - row - ing heart "re - joice"— For the
cresc.
dead— It whis-pers my sor - row - ing heart "re - joice"— For the
pp
p
last sad tear is shed— The pain that is all but a
p
last sad tear is shed— The pain that is all but a
p
last sad tear is shed— The pain that is all but a
p
last sad tear is shed— The pain that is all but a
p
last sad tear is shed— The pain that is all but a
p
last sad tear is shed— The pain that is all but a

cresc.
f
pleas - ure will change For the pleas - ure that's all but pain, And
cresc.
f
pleas - ure will change For the pleas - ure that's all but pain, And
cresc.
f
pleas - ure will change For the pleas - ure that's all but pain, And
cresc.
f
pleas - ure will change For the pleas - ure that's all but pain, And
cresc.
f
pleas - ure will change For the pleas - ure that's all but pain, And
cresc.
f
pleas - ure will change For the pleas - ure that's all but pain, And
f dim.
dim.
nev - er, oh, nev - er, our hearts will range From that old, old love a -
dim.
nev - er, oh, nev - er, our hearts will range From that old, old love a -
dim.
nev - er, oh, nev - er, our hearts will range From that old, old love a -
dim.
nev - er, oh, nev - er, our hearts will range From that old, old love a -
dim.
nev - er, oh, nev - er, our hearts will range From that old, old love a -
dim.
nev - er, oh, nev - er, our hearts will range From that old, old love a -

B
p
cresc.
gain! Yes, the pain that is all but a pleas - ure will change For the
gain! Yes, the pain that is all but a pleas - ure will change For the
gain! Yes, the pain that is all but a pleas - ure will change For the
gain! Yes, the pain that is all but a pleas - ure will change For the
gain! Yes, the pain that is all but a pleas - ure will change For the
gain! Yes, the pain that is all but a pleas - ure will change For the
Chorus
Yes, the pain that is all but a pleas - ure will change For the
Yes, the pain that is all but a pleas - ure will change For the
B
p

f
pleas - ure that's all but pain, And nev - er, oh, nev - er our
f
pleas - ure that's all but pain, And nev - er, oh, nev - er our
f
pleas - ure that's all but pain, And nev - er, oh, nev - er our
f
pleas - ure that's all but pain, And nev - er, oh, nev - er our
f
pleas - ure that's all but pain, And nev - er, oh, nev - er our
f
pleas - ure that's all but pain, And nev - er, oh, nev - er our
f
pleas - ure that's all but pain, And nev - er, oh, nev - er our
f
pleas - ure that's all but pain, And nev - er, oh, nev - er our
f dim.

C
dim.
hearts will range From that old, old love a - gain!
dim.
hearts will range From that old, old love a - gain!
dim.
hearts will range From that old, old love a - gain!
dim.
f
hearts will range From that old, old love a - gain! Oh,
dim.
hearts will range From that old, old love a - gain!
dim.
hearts will range From that old, old love a - gain!
dim.
hearts will range From that old, old love a - gain! Oh, nev - er, oh,
dim.
hearts will range From that old, old love a - gain! Oh, nev - er, oh,
C
pp

nev - - er, Oh, nev - - er our hearts will ___
nev - er our hearts, our hearts will range From that old, old love a -
nev - er our hearts, our hearts will range From that old, old love a -

f
Oh, nev - - er, oh, nev - er, our hearts will
f
Oh, nev - - er, oh, nev - er, our hearts will
f
Oh, nev - - er, oh,— nev - er, our hearts will
f
range, Oh, nev - - er, oh, nev - er, our hearts will
f
Oh, nev - - er, oh, nev - er, our hearts will
f
Oh, nev - - er, oh, nev - er, our hearts will
cresc.
gain! Oh, nev - er, oh, nev - er our hearts, oh,— nev - er, our hearts will
cresc.
gain! Oh, nev - er, oh, nev - er our hearts, oh, nev - er, our hearts will

dim.
p
range From that old, old love a - gain!
dim.
p
range From that old, old love a - gain!
dim.
p
range From that old, old love a - gain!
dim.
p
range From that old, old love a - gain!
dim.
p
range From that old, old love a - gain!
dim.
p
range From that old, old love a - gain!
f
dim.
p
range From that old, old love a - gain!
f
dim.
p
range From that old, old love a - gain!

(The Girls embrace the Officers. Re-enter Patience and Bunthorne, L.)

D
p a tempo

(As the Dragoons and Girls are embracing, enter Grosvenor, R.U.E., reading. He takes no notice of them, but comes slowly down, still reading. The Girls are strangely fascinated by him. The Chorus divides, L. & R., and the Girls are held back by the Dragoons, as they attempt to throw themselves at Grosvenor. Fury of Bunthorne, who recognizes a rival.)

E
Angela (R.C.)*
But who is this, whose god-like grace Pro-claims he comes of no-ble
race? And who is this, whose man-ly face Bears sor-row's in-ter-est-ing

*Because of the low range of this phrase, the Editor suggests that it be sung by Jane, Angela entering with "And who is this".

trace?
Chorus
Yes, who is this, whose god-like grace Pro-claims he comes of no-ble race?
Yes, who is this, whose god-like grace Pro-claims he comes of no-ble race?
F
Recit.
Grosvenor (C.)
I am a bro - ken-heart - ed trou - ba - dour, Whose
mind's æs - thet - ic and whose tastes are pure!

G
Vivace ♩= 160
Recit. Angela
Aes - thet - ic! He is æs - thet - ic!
f
dim.
p
Grosvenor
Yes, yes— I am æs - thet - ic And po - et - ic!
a tempo
Maidens
Then, we

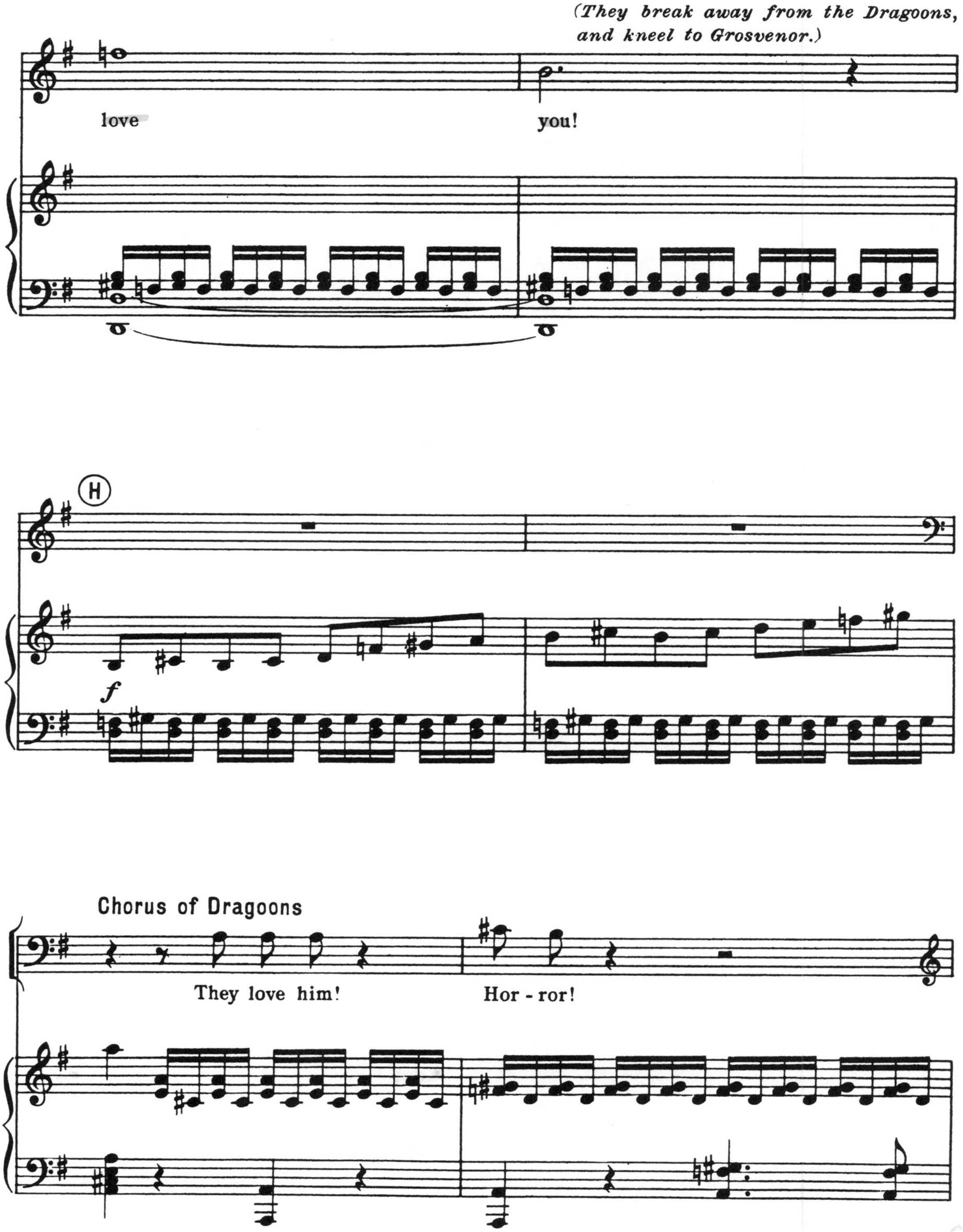
(They break away from the Dragoons, and kneel to Grosvenor.)
love
you!
H
f
Chorus of Dragoons
They love him!
Hor - ror!

Patience & Bunthorne
They love him!
Hor - ror!
cresc.
Grosvenor
They love me!
Hor - ror!
Hor - ror!
Hor-ror!
f
cresc.
molto

Allegretto agitato ♩= 160
Patience
List, Reg - i-nald, while I con-fess A
Ella
Oh, list while we a love con-fess That
Saphir
Oh, list while we a love con-fess That
Angela
Oh, list while we a love con-fess That
Jane
Oh, list while we a love con-fess That
Duke
My jeal - ous-y I can't ex-press, Their
Chorus
SOPRANO & ALTO
f
Oh, list while we a
TENOR & BASS
f
Oh, list while they a
Allegretto agitato ♩= 160
f

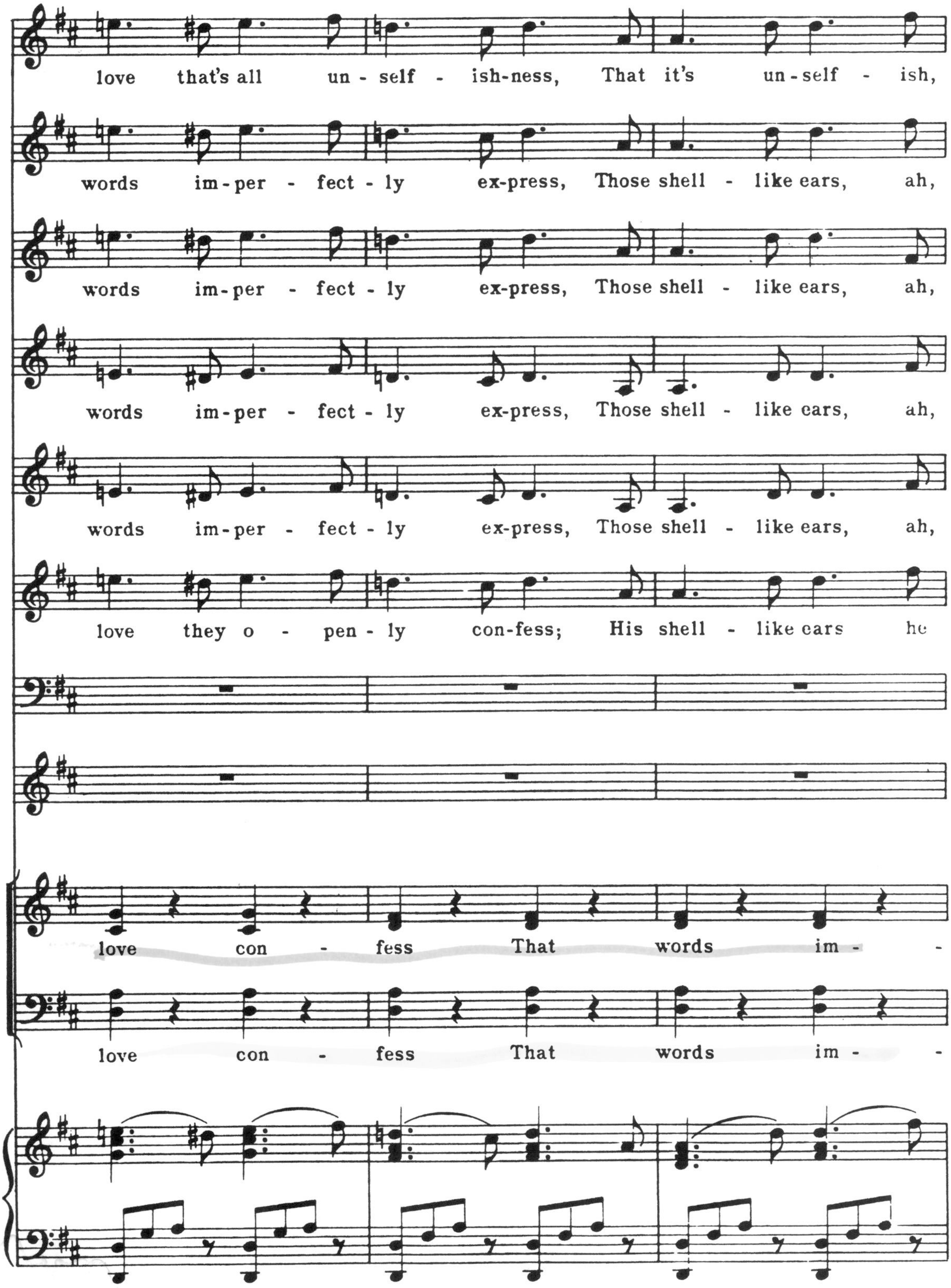
love that's all un - self - ish-ness, That it's un-self - ish,
words im-per - fect - ly ex-press, Those shell - like ears, ah,
words im-per - fect - ly ex-press, Those shell - like ears, ah,
words im-per - fect - ly ex-press, Those shell - like ears, ah,
words im-per - fect - ly ex-press, Those shell - like ears, ah,
love they o - pen - ly con-fess; His shell - like ears he
love con - fess That words im - -
love con - fess That words im - -

good - ness knows, You won't dis - pute it, I__ sup - pose!
do not close To blight - ed love's dis - tract - ing woes!
do not close To blight - ed love's dis - tract - ing woes!
do not close To blight - ed love's dis - tract - ing woes!
do not close To blight - ed love's dis - tract - ing woes!
does not close To their re - ci - tal of__ their woes!
Major & Colonel
My
Bunthorne
Grosvenor
My
A -
per - fect - ly ex - press! Yes, those
per - fect - ly ex - press! Yes, his

jeal - ous - y I can't ex - press, Their love they o - pen-
jeal - ous - y I can't ex - press, Their love they o - pen-
gain my curs - ed come - li - ness Spreads hope - less an - guish
shell - like ears, ah, do not close To blight - ed love's dis-
shell - like ears he does not close To their re - ci - tal

ly con - fess! Their love they o - pen - ly con-fess, con -
ly con - fess! Their love they o - pen - ly con-fess, con -
and dis - tress, Spreads hope - less an - guish and dis-tress, dis -
tract - ing woes! To blight - ed love's dis - tract - ing woes, its
of their woes! To their re - ci - tal of their woes, their

K
cresc.
p
Ah!
f
Oh, list while we our
Oh, list while we our
Oh, list while we our
Oh, list while we our
p
cresc.
Ah!
fess! My jeal - ous - y I
fess! My jeal - ous - y I
tress! A - gain my curs - ed
woes! Oh, list while we a
woes! Oh, list while they a
K

ff
And
ff
love con-fess That words im-per - fect - ly ex-press. Thy
ff
love con-fess That words im-per - fect - ly ex-press. Thy
ff
love con-fess That words im-per - fect - ly ex-presc. Thy
ff
love con-fess That words im-per - fect - ly ex-press. Thy
ff
His
can't ex-press, Their love they o - pen - ly con-fess. His
can't ex-press, Their love they o - pen - ly con-fess. His
come - li-ness Spreads hope - less an - guish and dis-tress; Thine
love con-fess That words im-per - fect - ly ex-press. Those
love con-fess That words im-per - fect - ly ex-press. His
ff

I shall love you, I shall love. Your ears, ah, do not
shell - like ears, ah, do not close To love's dis - tract - ing
shell - like ears, ah, do not close To love's dis - tract - ing
shell - like ears, ah, do not close To love's dis - tract - ing
shell - like ears, ah, do not close To love's dis - tract - ing
shell - like ears he does not close To love's dis - tract - ing
shell - like ears he does not close To love's dis-tract - ing
shell - like ears he does not close To love's dis-tract - ing
ears, oh, For - tune, do not close To love's dis-tract - ing
shell - like ears ah, do not close To love's dis-tract - ing
shell - like ears He does not close To love's dis-tract - ing

L
close! Thy shell - like ears, ah, do not
woes! Thy shell - like ears, ah, do not
woes! Thy shell - like ears, ah, do not
woes! Thy shell - like ears, ah, do not
woes! Thy shell - like ears, ah, do not
woes! His shell - like ears he does not
woes! Now is not this ri - dic - u - lous, and is not this pre -
woes! His shell - like ears he does not
woes! My shell - like ears I can - not
woes! Those shell - like ears, ah, do not
woes! Now is not this ri - dic - u - lous, and is not this pre -
L

close To blight - ed love's dis - tract - ing
close To blight - ed love's dis - tract - ing
close To blight - ed love's dis - tract - ing
close To blight - ed love's dis - tract - ing
close To blight - ed love's dis - tract - ing
close To blight - - ed love's dis - tract - ing
pos-ter - ous? A thor-ough-paced ab - surd - i - ty, ex-plain it if you
close To blight - ed love's dis - tract - ing
close To blight - ed love's dis - tract - ing
close To blight - ed love's dis - tract - ing
pos-ter - ous? A thor-ough-paced ab - surd - i - ty, ex-plain it if you

woes! Thy shell - like ears, ah, do not
woes! Thy shell - like ears, ah, do not
woes! Thy shell - like ears, ah, do not
woes! Thy shell - like ears, ah, do not
woes! Thy shell - like ears, ah, do not
woes! His shell - like ears he does not
can! Now is not this ri - dic - u - lous, and is not this pre -
woes! His shell - like ears he does not
woes! My shell - like ears I can - not
woes! Those shell - like ears, ah, do not
can! Now is not this ri - dic - u - lous, and is not this pre -

close To blight - ed love's dis - tract - ing
close To blight - ed love's dis - tract - ing
close To blight - ed love's dis - tract - ing
close To blight - ed love's dis - tract - ing
close To blight - ed love's dis - tract - ing
close To blight - ed love's dis - tract - ing
pos-ter-ous? A thor-ough-paced ab - surd-i - ty, ex-plain it if you
close To blight - ed love's dis - tract - ing
close To blight - ed love's dis - tract - ing
pos-ter-ous? A thor-ough-paced ab - surd-i - ty, ex-plain it if you

woes! To love's, to love's dis - tract - ing
woes! To love's, to love's dis - tract - ing
woes! To love's, to love's dis - tract - ing
woes! To love's, to love's dis - tract - ing
woes! To love's, to love's dis - tract - ing
woes! To love's, to love's dis - tract - ing
can! Ex - plain, ex - plain it if you
woes! To love's, to love's dis - tract - ing
woes! To love's, to love's dis - tract - ing
can! Ex - plain, ex - plain it if you

M
woes! love's woes!
woes! love's woes!
woes! love's woes!
woes! love's woes!
woes! love's woes!
woes! love's woes!
can! you can!
woes! love's woes!
(Grosvenor makes a wild effort to escape up-stage; the Girls drag him back and kneel as the curtain falls.)
woes! love's woes!
can! you can!
M
a tempo
ff

End of Act I

Act II

Scene: *A wooded glade, with a view of open country in the background. The Chorus of Maidens is heard singing in the distance. Jane is discovered leaning upon a violoncello, which she has propped up on a tree-stump, L., and upon which she will presently accompany herself. As the Chorus ends, she speaks.*

No. 10. On such eyes as maidens cherish

Opening Chorus

Maidens

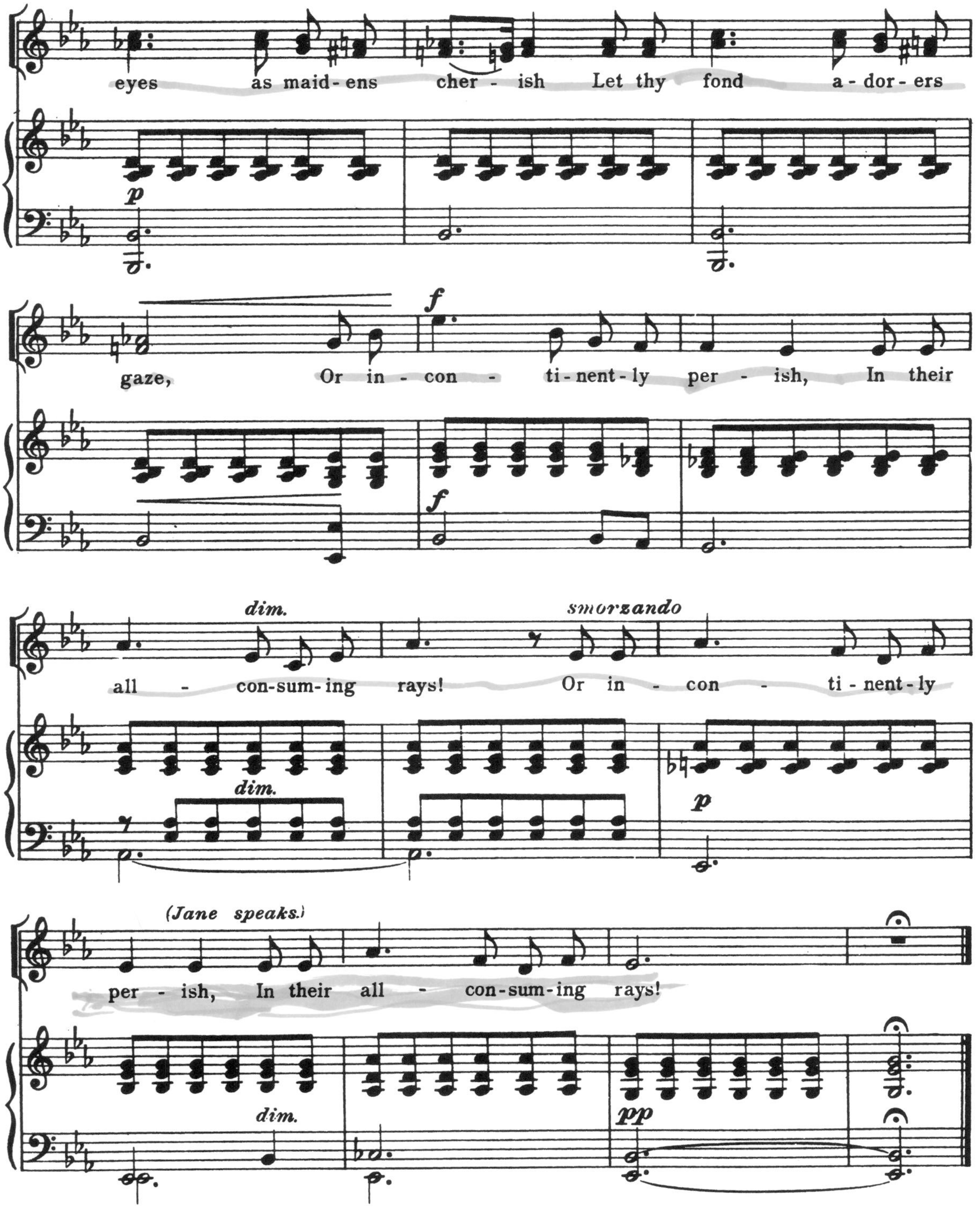
eyes as maid-ens cher-ish Let thy fond a-dor-ers
p
gaze, Or in-con-ti-nent-ly per-ish, In their
f
f
dim.
smorzando
all-con-sum-ing rays! Or in-con-ti-nent-ly
dim.
p
(Jane speaks.)
per-ish, In their all-con-sum-ing rays!
dim.
pp

Jane: The fickle crew have deserted Reginald and sworn allegiance to his rival, and all, forsooth, because he has glanced with passing favour on a puling milkmaid! Fools! Of that fancy he will soon weary — and then, I, who alone am faithful to him, shall reap my reward. But do not dally too long, Reginald, for my charms are ripe, Reginald, and already they are decaying. Better secure me ere I have gone too far!

No. 11. Sad is that woman's lot

Recitative and Solo

Jane

life's un-cer-tain gloam-ings, To wreathe her wrin-kled brow with well-saved
"comb-ings," Re-duced, with rouge, lip-shade, and pearl-y grey,
f
fz
fz
fz
dim.
To "make up" for lost time as best she may!
r. h.
Andante moderato ♩=88
Sil-vered is the ra - ven hair, Spread-ing is the part-ing straight,
p

Mot-tled the com-plex-ion fair, Halt-ing is the youth-ful gait, Hol-low is the
-rall.
a tempo
laugh-ter free, Spec-ta-cled the lim-pid eye, Lit-tle will be left of — me In the
a tempo
rall.
p
com-ing bye and bye! Lit-tle will be left of me In the com-ing bye and
mf
bye! Fad-ing is the
mf
p

ta - per waist, Shape-less grows the shape-ly limb, And al-though se - vere - ly laced,
Spread-ing is the_ fig - ure trim! Stout - er than I used to be, Still more cor-pu -
rall.
a tempo
lent grow I—__ There will be too much of_ me In the com-ing by and bye! There will be too
f
rall.
p a tempo
mf
appassionato
ff
(Exit, L., carrying her violoncello.)
much of me In the com - ing by and bye!
a tempo
f

(Enter Grosvenor, R., followed by Maidens, two and two, playing on archaic instruments as in Act I. He is reading abstractedly, as Bunthorne did in Act I, and pays no attention to them.)

No. 12. Turn, oh, turn in this direction

Chorus

Maidens

eyes as maid-ens cher - ish Let thy fond a - dor - ers
gaze, Or in - con - ti - nent - ly per - ish, In their
dim.
(Grosvenor sits, R.; they group themselves around him
all - con-sum-ing rays! Or in - con - ti - nent - ly
in a formation similar to that which opens Act I.)
per - ish, In their all - con-sum-ing rays!

Grosvenor: *(aside, not looking up)* The old, old tale! How rapturously these maidens love me, and how hopelessly! *(He looks up.)* Oh, Patience, Patience, with the love of thee in my heart, what have I for these poor mad maidens but an unvalued pity? Alas, they will die of hopeless love for me, as I shall die of hopeless love for thee!

Angela: Sir, will it please you read to us?

Grosvenor: *(sighing)* Yes, child, if you will. What shall I read?

Angela: One of your own poems.

Grosvenor: One of my own poems? Better not, my child. ***They*** will not cure thee of thy love. *(All sigh.)*

Ella: Mr. Bunthorne used to read us a poem of his own every day.

Saphir: And, to do him justice, he read them extremely well.

Grosvenor: Oh, did he so? Well, who am I that I should take upon myself to withhold my gifts from you? What am I but a trustee? Here is a decalet — a pure and simple thing, a very daisy — a babe might understand it. To appreciate it, it is not necessary to think of anything at all.

Angela: Let us think of nothing at all!

Grosvenor: *(reciting)*

Gentle Jane was as good as gold,
She always did as she was told;
She never spoke when her mouth was full,
Or caught bluebottles their legs to pull,
Or spilt plum jam on her nice new frock,
Or put white mice in the eight-day clock,
Or vivisected her last new doll,
Or fostered a passion for alcohol.
    And when she grew up she was given in marriage
    To a first - class earl who keeps his carriage!

Grosvenor: I believe I am right in saying that there is not one word in that decalet which is calculated to bring the blush of shame to the cheek of modesty.

Angela: Not one; it is purity itself.

Grosvenor: Here's another.

Teasing Tom was a very bad boy,
A great big squirt was his favourite toy,
He put live shrimps in his father's boots,
And sewed up sleeves of his Sunday suits;
He punched his poor little sisters' heads,
And cayenne - peppered their four - post beds;
He plastered their hair with cobbler's wax,
And dropped hot halfpennies down their backs.
The consequence was he was lost totally,
And married a girl in the *corps de bally!*

(The Maidens express intense horror.)

Angela: Marked you how grandly — how relentlessly — the damning catalogue of crime strode on, till Retribution, like a poised hawk, came swooping down upon the Wrong-Doer? Oh, it was terrible! *(All shudder.)*

Ella: Oh, sir, you are indeed a true poet, for you touch our hearts, and they go out to you!

Grosvenor: *(aside)* This is simply cloying. *(aloud)* Ladies, I am sorry to appear ungallant, but this is Saturday, and you have been following me about ever since Monday. I should like the usual half - holiday. I shall take it as a personal favour if you will kindly allow me to close early to-day.

Saphir: Oh, sir, do not send us from you!

Grosvenor: Poor, poor girls! It is best to speak plainly. I know that I am loved by you, but I never can love you in return, for my heart is fixed elsewhere! Remember the fable of the Magnet and the Churn.

Angela: *(wildly)* But we don't know the fable of the Magnet and the Churn!

Grosvenor: Don't you? Then I will sing it to you.

No. 13. A magnet hung in a hardware shop

Solo and Chorus

Grosvenor and Maidens

But for i-ron the mag-net felt no whim,
p
mf
Though he charm-ed i-ron, it charmed not him; From nee-dles and nails and
p
knives he'd turn, For he'd set his love on a Sil-ver
cre - scen - do
Chorus of Maidens
Grosvenor
Churn! A Sil-ver Churn! A
p

Sil- ver Churn! His_ most æs - thet- ic,_ Ve-ry mag-net - ic_
Fan- cy took this turn— "If I can whee-dle A knife or a nee-dle,
Why not a Sil- ver Churn?" His most æs - thet- ic,_ Ve-ry mag-net - ic_
Chorus of Maidens
Fan - cy took this turn— "If I can whee-dle A knife or nee-dle,

(He rises, going C.)
Why not a Sil - ver Churn?"
ff
Grosvenor
And I - ron and Steel ex - pressed sur-prise, The
p
nee-dles o-pened their well-drilled eyes, The pen-knives felt "shut up," no doubt, The
scis-sors de-clared them - selves "cut_ out".
mf

The ket-tles they boiled with rage, 'tis said,
p
mf
While ev-'ry nail went off its head, And hith-er and thith-er be-
p
gan to roam, Till a ham-mer came up and drove them
cre - scen - - do
home.
Chorus of Maidens
It drove them home?
Grosvenor
It
p

drove them home! While this mag-net-ic, Pe-ri-pa-tet-ic
Lov-er he lived to learn, By no en-deav-our Can mag-net ev-er At-
tract a Sil-ver Churn!
Chorus of Maidens
While this mag-net-ic, Pe-ri-pa-tet-ic
Chorus and Grosvenor
rall.
Lov-er he lived to learn, By no en-deav-our Can mag-net ev-er At-
rall.

(They go off in low spirits, R.U.E., gazing back
tract a Sil - ver Churn!
a tempo
ff
at him from time to time.)

Grosvenor: At last they are gone! What is this mysterious fascination that I seem to exercise over all I come across? A curse on my fatal beauty, for I am sick of conquests! *(Goes R.)*

(Enter Patience, L. Stops L.C. on seeing Grosvenor.)

Grosvenor: *(Turns and sees her.)* Patience!

Patience: I have escaped with difficulty from my Reginald. I wanted to see you so much that I might ask you if you still love me as fondly as ever?

Grosvenor: Love you? If the devotion of a lifetime—*(seizing her hand)*

Patience: *(indignantly)* Hold! Unhand me, or I scream! *(He releases her.)* If you are a gentleman, pray remember that I am another's! *(very tenderly)* But you *do* love me, don't you?

Grosvenor: Madly, hopelessly, despairingly!

Patience: That's right! I never can be yours; but that's right!

Grosvenor: And you love this Bunthorne?

Patience: With a heart-whole ecstasy that withers, and scorches, and burns, and stings! *(sadly)* It is my duty.

Grosvenor: Admirable girl! But you are not happy with him?

Patience: Happy? I am miserable beyond description!

Grosvenor: That's right! I never can be yours; but that's right!

Patience: But go now. I see dear Reginald approaching. Farewell, dear Archibald; I cannot tell you how happy it has made me to know that you still love me.

Grosvenor: Ah, if I only dared— *(advancing towards her)*

Patience: Sir! this language to one who is promised to another! *(tenderly)* Oh, Archibald, think of me sometimes, for my heart is breaking! He is so unkind to me, and you would be so loving!

Grosvenor: Loving! *(advancing toward her)*

Patience: Advance one step, and as I am a good and pure woman, I scream! *(tenderly)* Farewell, Archibald! *(sternly)* Stop there! *(tenderly)* Think of me sometimes! *(angrily)* Advance at your peril! Once more, adieu!

(Grosvenor sighs, gazes sorrowfully at her, sighs deeply, and exits, R. She bursts into tears.)

(Enter Bunthorne, followed by Jane. He is moody and preoccupied.)

Jane: *(singing)*

Allegretto
mf
In a dole-ful train One and one I walk all day; For I
sf
love in vain; None so sor-row-ful as they Who can on-ly
sigh and say, Woe is me, a-lack-a-day!

Bunthorne: *(seeing Patience)* Crying, eh? What are you crying about?

Patience: I've only been thinking how dearly I love you!

Bunthorne: Love me! Bah!

Jane: Love him! Bah!

Bunthorne: *(to Jane)* Don't you interfere.

Jane: He always crushes me!

Patience: *(going to him)* What is the matter, dear Reginald? If you have any sorrow, tell it to me, that I may share it with you. *(sighing)* It is my duty!

Bunthorne: *(snappishly)* Whom were you talking with just now?

Patience: With dear Archibald.

Bunthorne: *(furiously)* With dear Archibald! Upon my honour, this is too much!

Jane: A great deal too much!

Bunthorne: *(angrily to Jane)* Do be quiet!

Jane: Crushed again!

Patience: I think he is the noblest, purest, and most perfect being I have ever met. But I don't love him. It is true that he is devotedly attached to me, but I don't love *him.* Whenever he grows affectionate, I scream. It is my duty! *(sighing)*

Bunthorne: I dare say.

Jane: So do I! *I* dare say!

Patience: Why, how could I love him and love you too? You can't love two people at once!

Bunthorne: Oh, can't you though!

Patience: No, you can't; I only wish you could.

Bunthorne: I don't believe you know what love is!

Patience: *(sighing)* Yes, I do. There was a happy time when I didn't, but a bitter experience has taught me.

(Bunthorne, noticing that Jane is not looking at him, goes off quickly up R. She turns, sees him, and runs after him.)

No. 14. Love is a plaintive song

Solo

Patience

rall.
mote, Mer - ry when he is glad! Mer - ry when he is glad!
him, Noth - ing at all for her! Noth - ing at all for her!
rall.
a tempo
Love that no wrong can cure, Love that is al - ways new,
Love that will aye en - dure, Though the re - wards be few,
a tempo
p
That is the love that's pure, That is the love that's true!
That is the love that's pure, That is the love that's true!
Love that no wrong can cure, Love that is al - ways new,
Love that will aye en - dure, Though the re - wards be few,
cre - scen - do

That is the love_ that's pure, That ______ is_ the love,_ the
f
ad lib.
love_ that's true! ___
colla voce
f
a tempo

(At the end of the Ballad exit Patience, L., weeping. Enter Bunthorne, R., Jane following.)

Bunthorne: Everything has gone wrong with me since that smug-faced idiot came here. Before that I was admired – I may say, loved.

Jane: Too mild – adored!

Bunthorne: Do let a poet soliloquize! The damozels used to follow me wherever I went; now they all follow him!

Jane: Not all! *I* am still faithful to you.

Bunthorne: Yes, and a pretty damozel *you* are!

Jane: No, not pretty. Massive. Cheer up! I will never leave you, I swear it!

Bunthorne: Oh, thank you! I know what it is; it's his confounded mildness. They find me too highly spiced, if you please! And no doubt I *am* highly spiced.

Jane: Not for my taste!

Bunthorne: *(savagely)* No, but I am for theirs. But I will show the world I can be as mild as he. If they want insipidity, they shall have it. I'll meet this fellow on his own ground and beat him on it.

Jane: You shall. And I will help you.

Bunthorne: You will? Jane, there's a good deal of good in you, after all!

No. 15. So go to him and say to him

Duet

Jane and Bunthorne

Jane
ron - i - cal—
1st Verse Bunthorne
Sing "Hey to you-Good day to you"-And that's what I shall
2nd Verse Jane
Sing "Booh to you-Pooh, pooh to you"-And that's what you should
Bunthorne
joc - u - lar—
"Your style is much too sanc - ti - fied-your cut is too can -
say!
say!
To cut his cur - ly hair, and stick an eye-glass in his

on - i - cal"—
Sing "Bah to you— Ha! ha! to you"— And
Sing "Bah to you— Ha! ha! to you"— And
oc - u - lar —
"I was the beau i - de - al of the
that's what I shall say!
that's what you should say!
To stuff his con-ver - sa - tion full of

mor - bid young æs - thet - i - cal— To doubt my in - spi -
quib - ble and of quid - di - ty, To dine on chops and
ra - tion was re - gard - ed as he - ret - i - cal— Un -
ro - ly - po - ly pud - ding with a - vid - i - ty— He'd

til you cut me out with your pla - cid - i - ty e -
better clear a - way with all con - ven - i - ent ra -
met - i - cal."
Sing "Booh to you— pooh, pooh to you"— and
Sing "Hey to you— good day to you"— and
pid - i - ty.

that's what I shall say! Sing "Booh to you–pooh, pooh to you"– and
that's what you should say!
Sing "Booh to you–pooh, pooh to you"– and
Sing "Hey to you–good -
that's what I shall say! "Hey,
Sing "Hey to you–good -
that's what I shall say! "Hey,
pp

day to you"– Sing "Bah to you— ha! ha! to you"– Sing
1st Verse
Good - day,
day to you"–Sing "Bah to you— ha! ha! to you"– Sing
2nd Verse
Good - day,
"Booh to you—pooh, pooh to you"—And that's what you should
Bah, ha! ha!
"Booh to you—pooh, pooh to you"—And that's what you should
Bah, ha! ha!
f

say! Sing "Hey to you-good - day to you"-Sing "Bah to you- ha!
Booh, pooh, pooh,
say! Sing "Hey to you-good - day to you"-Sing "Bah to you- ha!
Booh, pooh, pooh,
pp
ha! to you," Sing "Booh to you"- And that's what you should
Bah," And that's what I shall
cresc.
say! "Bah, bah," And that's what you should
say! "Booh, booh," And that's what I shall
f
p

say! "Booh, booh," And that's what
say! "Bah, bah," And that's what
cre - - scen - do
Upper notes and 𝄐 2nd Verse
you should say!
I shall say!
𝄐 2nd Verse
f
ff
(They dance off, L.)

(Enter Duke, Colonel, and Major, R. They have abandoned their uniforms, and are dressed and made up in imitation of Aesthetics. They have long hair, and other signs of attachment to the brotherhood. As they sing they walk in stiff, constrained, and angular attitudes — a grotesque exaggeration of the attitudes adopted by Bunthorne and the young Ladies in Act I.)

No. 16. It's clear that mediæval art

Trio

Duke, Major, and Colonel

(Enter Duke . . . . . enter Major . . . . . enter Colonel,
Andante ♩ = 72
p
(Attitude)
(They walk to C.)
Duke
1. It's clear that me - di - æ - val art a - lone re - tains its
2. If this is not ex - act - ly right, we hope you won't up -
Major
1. It's clear that me - di - æ - val art a - lone re - tains its
2. If this is not ex - act - ly right, we hope you won't up -
Colonel
1. It's clear that me - di - æ - val art a - lone re - tains its
2. If this is not ex - act - ly right, we hope you won't up -

zest, To charm and please its dev - o-tees we've done our lit - tle
braid; You can't get high Aes-thet - ic tastes like trou - sers, read - y
zest, To charm and please its dev - o-tees we've done our lit - tle
braid; You can't get high Aes-thet - ic tastes like trou - sers, read - y
zest, To charm and please its dev - o-tees we've done our lit - tle
braid; You can't get high Aes-thet - ic tastes like trou - sers, read - y
best. We're not quite sure if all we do has the Ear - ly Eng - lish
made. True views on Me - di - æ - val-is - m, Time a-lone will
best. We're not quite sure if all we do has the Ear - ly Eng - lish
made. True views on Me - di - æ - val-is - m, Time a-lone will
best. We're not quite sure if all we do has the Ear - ly Eng - lish
made. True views on Me - di - æ - val-is - m, Time a-lone will

ring; But, as far as we can judge, it's some - thing like this sort of
bring,
ring; But, as far as we can judge, it's some - thing like this sort of
bring,
ring; But, as far as we can judge, it's some - thing like this sort of
bring,
(attitude)
thing: You hold your-self like this, You
thing: You hold your-self like this, You
thing: You hold your-self like this, You

(attitude)
hold your-self like that, By hook and crook you try to look both
hold your-self like that, By hook and crook you try to look both
hold your-self like that, By hook and crook you try to look both
an - gu-lar and flat. We ven - ture to ex - pect That
To cul - ti - vate the trim Ri -
an - gu-lar and flat. We ven - ture to ex - pect That
To cul - ti - vate the trim Ri -
an - gu-lar and flat. We ven - ture to ex - pect That
To cul - ti - vate the trim Ri -

what we re - col - lect, Though but a part of true High Art, will
gid - i - ty of limb, You ought to get a Mar - io-nette, and
what we re - col - lect, Though but a part of true High Art, will
gid - i - ty of limb, You ought to get a Mar - io-nette, and
what we re - col - lect, Though but a part of true High Art, will
gid - i - ty of limb, You ought to get a Mar - io-nette, and
have its due ef - fect.
form your style on him.
have its due ef - fect.
form your style on him.
have its due ef - fect.
form your style on him.
(Attitudes change in time to the music.)
p

Colonel: *(attitude)* Yes, it's quite clear that our only chance of making a lasting impression on these young ladies is to become as aesthetic as they are.

Major: *(attitude)* No doubt. The only question is how far we've succeeded in doing so. I don't know why, but I've an idea that this is not quite right.

Duke: *(attitude)* *I* don't like it. I never did. I don't see what it means. I do it, but I don't like it.

Colonel: My good friend, the question is not whether we like it, but whether they do. They understand these things — we don't. Now I shouldn't be surprised if this is effective enough — at a distance.

Major: I can't help thinking we're a little stiff at it. It would be extremely awkward if we were to be "struck" so!

Colonel: I don't think we shall be struck so. Perhaps we're a little awkward at first — but everything must have a beginning. Oh here they come! 'Tention!

(They strike fresh attitudes, as Angela and Saphir enter, L.)

Angela: *(seeing them)* Oh, Saphir — see — see! The immortal fire has descended on them, and they are of the Inner Brotherhood — perceptively intense and consummately utter. *(The Officers have some difficulty in maintaining their constrained attitudes.)*

Saphir: *(in admiration)* How Botticelian! How Fra Angelican! Oh, Art, we thank thee for this boon!

Colonel: *(apologetically)* I'm afraid we're not quite right.

Angela: Not supremely, perhaps, but oh, so all — but! *(to Saphir)* Oh, Saphir, are they not quite too all — but?

Saphir: They are indeed jolly utter!

Major: *(in agony)* I wonder what the Inner Brotherhood usually recommend for cramp?

Colonel: Ladies, we will not deceive you. We are doing this at some personal inconvenience with a view of expressing the extremity of our devotion to you. We trust that it is not without its effect.

Angela: We will not deny that we are much moved by this proof of your attachment.

Saphir: Yes, your conversion to the principles of Aesthetic Art in its highest development has touched us deeply.

Angela: And if Mr. Grosvenor should remain obdurate —

Saphir: Which we have every reason to believe he will —

Major: *(aside, in agony)* I wish they'd make haste! *(The others hush him.)*

Angela: We are not prepared to say that our yearning hearts will not go out to you.

Colonel: *(as giving a word of command)* By sections of threes — Rapture! *(All strike a fresh attitude, expressive of æsthetic rapture.)*

Saphir: Oh, it's extremely good — for beginners it's admirable!

Major: The only question is, who will take who?

Colonel: Oh, the Duke chooses first, as a matter of course.

Duke: Oh, I couldn't think of it — you are really too good!

Colonel: Nothing of the kind. You are a great matrimonial fish, and it's only fair that each of these ladies should have a chance of hooking you. It's perfectly simple. Observe, suppose you choose Angela, I take Saphir, Major takes nobody. *(with increasing speed)* Suppose you choose Saphir, Major takes Angela, I take nobody. Suppose you choose neither, I take Angela, Major takes Saphir. Clear as day!

No. 17. If Saphir I choose to marry

Quintet

Duke, Colonel, Major, Angela, and Saphir

(The Officers, with obvious relief, abandon their aesthetic attitudes, and, with the Ladies, dance into position.

L. to R. 1st verse: Colonel with Angela; Duke with Saphir; Major alone.
2nd verse: Colonel alone; Angela with Duke; Saphir with Major.
3rd verse: Colonel with Saphir; Duke alone; Angela with Major.)

Allegretto ♩. = 112
ff
p
Duke
1. If Sa-phir I choose to mar - ry, I shall be fixed up for
2. If on An - gy I de - ter - mine, At my wed - ding she'll ap -

life; Then the Col - onel need not tar - ry, An - ge - la can be his
pear, Decked in di - a - mond and er - mine. Ma - jor then can take Sa -
Major 1st Verse
wife. In that case un - prec - e - dent - ed, Sin - gle I shall live and
phir!
Colonel 2nd Verse
In that case un - prec - e - dent - ed, Sin - gle I shall live and
die — I shall have to be con - tent - ed With their heart - felt sym - pa -
die — I shall have to be con - tent - ed With their heart - felt sym - pa -

Saphir
He — will have to be con - tent - ed With — our heart - felt sym - pa -
Angela
He — will have to be con - tent - ed With — our heart - felt sym - pa -
Duke
He will have to be con - tent - ed With our heart - felt sym - pa -
Major
thy! to be con - tent - ed With their heart - felt sym - pa -
2nd V. our heart - felt sym - pa -
Colonel
1st V. He will have to be con - tent - ed With our heart - felt sym - pa -
2nd V. thy! I shall have to be con - tent - ed With their heart - felt sym - pa -
thy! In that
thy! In that
thy! In that
thy! In that
thy! In that
thy! In that
thy! In that

case un-prec - e - dent - ed, Sin - gle he will live and die — He will
case un-prec - e - dent - ed, Sin - gle he will live and die — He will
case un-prec - e - dent - ed, Sin - gle he will live and die — He will
case un-prec - e - dent - ed, Sin - gle I shall live and die — I shall
case un-prec - e - dent - ed, Sin - gle he will live and die — He will
case un-prec - e - dent - ed, Sin - gle he will live and die — he will
case un-prec - e - dent - ed, Sin - gle I shall live and die — I shall
have to be con - tent - ed With our heart - felt sym - pa - thy! He will
have to be con - tent - ed With our heart - felt sym - pa - thy! He will
have to be con - tent - ed With our heart - felt sym - pa - thy! He will
have to be con - tent - ed With their heart - felt sym - pa - thy! I shall
have to be con - tent - ed With our heart - felt sym - pa - thy! He will
have to be con - tent - ed With our heart - felt sym - pa - thy! He will
have to be con - tent - ed With their heart - felt sym - pa - thy! I shall
f

have to be con - tent - ed With our heart - felt sym - pa - thy! He will
have to be con - tent - ed With our heart - felt sym - pa - thy! He will
have to be con - tent - ed With our heart - felt sym - pa - thy! He will
have to be con - tent - ed With their heart - felt sym - pa - thy! I shall
have to be con - tent - ed With our heart - felt sym - pa - thy! He will
have to be con - tent - ed With our heart - felt sym - pa - thy! He will
have to be con - tent - ed With their heart - felt sym - pa - thy! I shall
have to be con - tent - ed With our heart - felt sym - pa - thy!
have to be con - tent - ed With our heart - felt sym - pa - thy!
have to be con - tent - ed With our heart - felt sym - pa - thy!
have to be con - tent - ed With their heart - felt sym - pa - thy!
have to be con - tent - ed With our heart - felt sym - pa - thy!
have to be con - tent - ed With our heart - felt sym - pa - thy!
have to be con - tent - ed With their heart - felt sym - pa - thy!
ff

(Positions at beginning of Verse 3:
L. to R., Colonel, Angela, Duke, Saphir, Major)
p
Duke
3. Af - ter some de-bate in - ter - nal, If on neith - er I de -
(Hands her to the Major.)
cide, Sa - phir then can take the Col - onel, An - gy be the Ma - jor's

bride! In that case un-prec-e-dent-ed, Sin-gle I must live and
die— I shall have to be con-tent-ed With their heart-felt sym-pa-
rall.
colla voce
Saphir
p a tempo
He — will have to be con-tent-ed With our heart-felt sym-pa-
Angela
p
He — will have to be con-tent-ed With our heart-felt sym-pa-
thy! to be con-tent-ed With their heart-felt sym-pa-
Major
p
He will have to be con-tent-ed With our heart-felt sym-pa-
Colonel
He will have to be con-tent-ed With our heart-felt sym-pa-
p a tempo

p
thy! In that
thy! In that
thy! In that
thy! In that
thy! In that
case un-prec - e - dent - ed, Sin - gle he will live and die, He will
case un-prec - e - dent - ed, Sin - gle he will live and die, He will
case un-prec - e - dent - ed, Sin - gle I shall live and die, I shall
case un-prec - e - dent - ed, Sin - gle he will live and die, He will
case un-prec - e - dent - ed, Sin - gle he will live and die, He will

have to be con - tent - ed With our heart - felt sym - pa - thy! He will
have to be con - tent - ed With our heart - felt sym - pa - thy! He will
have to be con - tent - ed With their heart - felt sym - pa - thy! I shall
have to be con - tent - ed With our heart - felt sym - pa - thy! He will
have to be con - tent - ed With our heart - felt sym - pa - thy! He will
have to be con - tent - ed With our heart - felt sym - pa - thy! He will
have to be con - tent - ed With our heart - felt sym - pa - thy! He will
have to be con - tent - ed With their heart - felt sym - pa - thy! I shall
have to be con - tent - ed With our heart - felt sym - pa - thy! He will
have to be con - tent - ed With our heart - felt sym - pa - thy! He will

ff
have to be con-tent-ed With our heart - felt sym - pa-thy!
ff
have to be con-tent-ed With our heart - felt sym - pa-thy!
ff
have to be con-tent-ed With their heart - felt sym - pa-thy!
ff
have to be con-tent-ed With our heart - felt sym - pa-thy!
ff
have to be con-tent-ed With our heart - felt sym - pa-thy!
ff a tempo
(They dance off, arm-in-arm, up-stage and off, L.U.E., the Colonel leading with
Saphir.)
ffz
ffz

(Enter Grosvenor, R.U.E.)

Grosvenor: It is very pleasant to be alone. It is pleasant to be able to gaze at leisure upon those features which all others may gaze upon at their good will! *(looking at his reflection in a hand mirror)* Ah, I am a very Narcissus!

(Enter Bunthorne, L. moodily.)

Bunthorne: It's no use; I can't live without admiration. Since Grosvenor came here, insipidity has been at a premium. Ah, he is there!

Grosvenor: Ah, Bunthorne! Come here — look! Very graceful, isn't it?

Bunthorne: *(taking the hand-mirror)* Allow me; I haven't seen it. Yes, it is graceful.

Grosvenor: *(taking back the mirror)* Oh, good gracious! Not that — this —

Bunthorne: You don't mean *that!* Bah! I am in no mood for trifling.

Grosvenor: And what is amiss?

Bunthorne: Ever since you came here, you have entirely monopolized the attentions of the young ladies. I don't like it, sir!

Grosvenor: My dear sir, how can I help it? They are the plague of my life. My dear Mr. Bunthorne, with your personal disadvantages, you can have no idea of the inconvenience of being madly loved, at first sight, by every woman you meet.

Bunthorne: Sir, until you came here I was adored!

Grosvenor: Exactly — until I came here. That's my grievance. I cut everybody out! I assure you, if you could only suggest some means whereby, consistently with my duty to society, I could escape these inconvenient attentions, you would earn my everlasting gratitude.

Bunthorne: I will do so at once. However popular it may be with the world at large, your personal appearance is highly objectionable to *me.*

Grosvenor: It is? *(shaking his hand)* Oh, thank you! thank you! How can I express my gratitude?

Bunthorne: By making a complete change at once. Your conversation must henceforth be perfectly matter-of-fact. You must cut your hair, and have a back parting. In appearance and costume you must be absolutely commonplace.

Grosvenor: *(decidedly)* No. Pardon me, that's impossible.

Bunthorne: Take care! When I am thwarted I am very terrible.

Grosvenor: *(crossing to R.)* I can't help that. I am a man with a mission. And that mission must be fulfilled.

Bunthorne: I don't think you quite appreciate the consequences of thwarting me.

Grosvenor: I don't care what they are.

Bunthorne: Suppose — I won't go so far as to say that I will do it – but suppose for one moment I were to curse you! *(Grosvenor quails.)* Ah! Very well. Take care.

Grosvenor: But surely you would never do that? *(in great alarm)*

Bunthorne: I don't know. It would be an extreme measure, no doubt. Still —

Grosvenor: *(wildly)* But you would not do it – I am sure you would not. *(throwing himself at Bunthorne's knees, and clinging to him)* Oh, reflect, reflect! You had a mother once.

Bunthorne: Never!

Grosvenor: Then you had an aunt! *(Bunthorne is affected.)* Ah! I see you had! By the memory of that aunt, I implore you to pause ere you resort to this last fearful expedient. Oh, Mr. Bunthorne, reflect, reflect! *(weeping)*

Bunthorne: *(aside, after a struggle with himself)* I must not allow myself to be unmanned! *(aloud)* It is useless. Consent at once, or may a nephew's curse —

Grosvenor: Hold! Are you absolutely resolved?

Bunthorne: Absolutely!

Grosvenor: Will nothing shake you?

Bunthorne: Nothing. I am adamant!

Grosvenor: Very good. *(rising)* Then I yield.

Bunthorne: Ha! You swear it?

Grosvenor: I do, cheerfully. I have long wished for a reasonable pretext for such a change as you suggest. It has come at last. I do it on compulsion!

Bunthorne: Victory! I triumph!

No. 18. When I go out of door

Duet

Bunthorne and Grosvenor

(Each one dances around the stage while the other is singing his solo verses.)

fore. I shall, with cul - tured taste, Dis - tin - guish gems from
paste, And "High did - dle did - dle" Will rank as an i - dyll, If
Grosvenor
A most in - tense young man, A
I pro - nounce it chaste! A most in - tense young man, A
soul - ful - eyed young man— An ul - tra - po - et - i - cal,
soul - ful - eyed young man— An ul - tra - po - et - i - cal,

su - per - aes - thet - i - cal, Out - of - the - way young man! Con -
su - per - aes - thet - i - cal, Out - of - the - way young man!
ceive me, if you can, An ev - 'ry - day young man: A
com-mon-place type, With a stick and a pipe, And a half - bred black - and -
tan; Who thinks sub - ur - ban "hops" More fun than "Mon - day

Pops,"— Who's fond of his din - ner, And does - n't get thin - ner On
bot - tled beer and chops. A com - mon-place young man— A
Grosvenor
Bunthorne
A com - mon-place young man— A
mat - ter - of - fact young man— A stead - y and sto - lid - y,
mat - ter - of - fact young man— A stead - y and sto - lid - y,
jol - ly Bank-hol - i - day, Ev - e - ry - day young man!
jol - ly Bank-hol - i - day, Ev - e - ry - day young man! A Jap - a-nese young

man— A blue-and-white young man— Fran-ces-ca da Ri-mi-ni,
Grosvenor
mi-mi-ny, pim-i-ny, Je-ne-sais-quoi young man. A
Chan-ce-ry Lane young man— A Som-er-set House young
man,— A ver-y de-lec-ta-ble, high-ly re-spec-ta-ble

Bunthorne
Three-pen-ny-bus young man! A pal-lid and thin young man— A
hag-gard and lank young man, A green-er-y-yal-ler-y,
Grosvenor
Gros-ve-nor Gal-ler-y, Foot-in-the grave young man! A
Sew-ell and Cross young man, A How-ell and James young man, A

push-ing young par - ti - cle—"What's the next ar - ti - cle?"—Wa - ter - loo House young
Grosvenor
man! Con-ceive me if you can, A mat - ter - of - fact young
Bunthorne
Con-ceive me if you can, A crotch-et - y, cracked young
man, An al - pha-bet - i - cal, a - rith-met - i - cal,
man, An ul - tra - po - et - i - cal, su - per - æs - thet - i - cal,

Ev - e - ry day young man! Con - ceive me, if you can, A
Out - of - the - way young man! Con - ceive me, if you can, A
mat - ter - of - fact young man, An al - pha - bet - i - cal,
crotch - et - y, cracked young man, An ul - tra - po - et - i - cal,
(Dances off, L. U. E.)
a - rith - met - i - cal, Ev - e - ry - day young man!
su - per - æs - thet - i - cal, Out - of - the - way young man!
fz
fz

Bunthorne: It's all right! I have committed my last act of ill-nature, and henceforth I'm a changed character. *(Dances about stage, humming the refrain of the last air. Enter Patience, L. She gazes in astonishment at him.)*

Patience: Reginald! Dancing! And — what in the world is the matter with you?

Bunthorne: Patience, I'm a changed man. Hitherto I've been gloomy, moody, fitful — uncertain in temper and selfish in disposition—

Patience: You have, indeed! *(sighing)*

Bunthorne: All that is changed. I have reformed. I have modelled myself upon Mr. Grosvenor. Henceforth I am mildly cheerful. My conversation will blend amusement with instruction. I shall still be æsthetic; but my æstheticism will be of the most pastoral kind.

Patience: Oh, Reginald! Is all this true?

Bunthorne: Quite true. Observe how amiable I am. *(assuming a fixed smile)*

Patience: But, Reginald, how long will this last?

Bunthorne: With occasional intervals for rest and refreshment, as long as I do.

Patience: Oh, Reginald, I'm so happy! Oh, dear, dear Reginald, I cannot express the joy I feel at this change. It will no longer be a duty to love you, but a pleasure — a rapture — an ecstasy!

Bunthorne: My darling! *(embracing her)*

Patience: But — oh, horror! *(recoiling from him)*

Bunthorne: What's the matter?

Patience: Is it quite certain that you have absolutely reformed — that you are henceforth a perfect being — utterly free from defect of any kind?

Bunthorne: It is quite certain. I have sworn it.

Patience: Then I never can be yours! *(crossing to R.C.)*

Bunthorne: Why not?

Patience: Love, to be pure, must be absolutely unselfish, and there can be nothing unselfish in loving so perfect a being as you have now become!

Bunthorne: But stop a bit! I don't want to change — I'll relapse — I'll be as I was — interrupted!

(Enter Grosvenor, L.U.E., followed by all the young Ladies, who are followed by the Chorus of Dragoons. He has had his hair cut, and is dressed in an ordinary suit and a bowler hat. They all dance cheerfully round the stage in marked contrast to their former languor.)

No. 19. I'm a Waterloo House young man

Solo and Chorus

Grosvenor and Maidens

Grosvenor
I'm a Wa - ter - loo House young
man, A Sew - ell and Cross young man, A
stead - y and sto - lid - y, jol - ly Bank - hol - i - day, Ev - e - ry - day young
man.
Chorus of Maidens
We're Swears and Wells young girls, We're

Ma-dame Lou-ise young girls, We're pret-ti-ly pat-ter-ing,
cheer-i-ly chat-ter-ing, Ev-e-ry-day young girls.
fz
fz

Bunthorne: *(C.)* Angela — Ella — Saphir — what — what does this mean?

Angela: *(R.)* It means that Archibald the All - Right cannot be all - wrong; and if the All - Right chooses to discard æstheticism, it proves that æstheticism ought to be discarded.

Patience: Oh, Archibald! Archibald! I'm shocked — surprised — horrified!

Grosvenor: *(L.C.)* I can't help it. I'm not a free agent. I do it on compulsion.

Patience: This is terrible. Go! I shall never set eyes on you again. But — oh, joy!

Grosvenor: *(L.C.)* What is the matter?

Patience: *(R.C.)* It is quite, quite certain that you will always be a common-place young man?

Grosvenor: Always — I have sworn it.

Patience: Why, then, there's nothing to prevent my loving you with all the fervour at my command!

Grosvenor: Why, that's true!

Patience: *(crossing to him)* My Archibald!

Grosvenor: My Patience! *(They embrace.)*

Bunthorne: Crushed again!

(Enter Jane, L.)

Jane: *(who is still aesthetic)* Cheer up! I am still here. I have never left you, and I never will!

Bunthorne: Thank you, Jane. After all, there's no denying it, you're a fine figure of a woman!

Jane: My Reginald!

Bunthorne: My Jane! *(They embrace.)*

Fanfare *(Enter, R., Colonel, Major, and Duke. They are again in uniform.)*

Colonel: Ladies, the Duke has at length determined to select a bride!

(General excitement)

Duke: *(R.)* I have a great gift to bestow. Approach, such of you as are truly lovely. *(All the girls come forward, bashfully, except Jane and Patience.)* In personal appearance you have all that is necessary to make a woman happy. In common fairness, I think I ought to choose the only one among you who has the misfortune to be distinctly plain. *(Girls retire disappointed.)* Jane!

Jane: *(leaving Bunthorne's arms)* Duke! *(Jane and Duke embrace. Bunthorne is utterly disgusted.)*

Bunthorne: Crushed again!

No. 20. After much debate internal

Finale of Act II

Ensemble

Duke (R.C.)
Af - ter much de-bate in - ter - nal, I on La - dy Jane de -
(Saphir pairs off with Colonel, R., Angela with Major, L.C., Ella with Solicitor, L.)
cide, Sa - phir now may take the Col' - nel, An - gy be the Ma - jor's
Bunthorne (C.)
bride! In that case un-prec - e - dent - ed, Sin - gle I must live and
die, I shall have to be con - tent - ed With a tu - lip or_ li -

(Bunthorne, C., takes a lily from his buttonhole and gazes affectionately at it.)

case un-prec - e - dent - ed, Sin - gle he must live and
case un-prec - e - dent - ed, Sin - gle he must live and
case un-prec - e - dent - ed, Sin - gle he must live and
case un-prec - e - dent - ed, Sin - gle I must live and
case un-prec - e - dent - ed, Sin - gle he must live and
case un-prec - e - dent - ed, Sin - gle he must live and
p
die, He will have to be con - tent - ed With a tu - lip or li -
die, He will have to be con - tent - ed With a tu - lip or li -
die, He will have to be con - tent - ed With a tu - lip or li -
die, I shall have to be con - tent - ed With a tu - lip or li -
die, He will have to be con - tent - ed With a tu - lip or li -
die, He will have to be con - tent - ed With a tu - lip or li -

f
ly! Great - ly pleased with one an - oth - er, To get mar - ried we — de -
ly! Great - ly pleased with one an - oth - er, To get mar - ried we de -
ly! Great - ly pleased with one an - oth - er, To get mar - ried we de -
ly! Great - ly pleased with one an - oth - er, To get mar - ried they de -
ly! Great - ly pleased with one an - oth - er, To get mar - ried we de -
ly! Great - ly pleased with one an - oth - er, To get mar - ried we — de -
cide, Each of us will wed the oth - er, No - bo - dy
cide, Each of us will wed the oth - er, No - bo - dy
cide, Each of us will wed the oth - er, No - bo - dy
cide, Each of them will wed the oth - er, No - bo - dy
cide, Each of us will wed the oth - er, No - bo - dy
cide, Each of us will wed the oth - er, No - bo - dy

ff
be Bun - thorne's Bride!
ff
be Bun - thorne's Bride!
ff
be Bun - thorne's Bride!
ff
be Bun - thorne's Bride!
ff
be Bun - thorne's Bride!
ff
be Bun - thorne's Bride!
ff
ff
fffz

End of Opera